# From Snowmen to Kangaroos:
## A Most Unlikely Journey

by BILL PETERSON

From Snowmen to Kangaroos: A Most Unlikely Journey
© Bill Peterson 2022

All rights reserved. No part of this publication may be reproduced, stored in a retrieval system, or transmitted in any form or by any means, electronic, mechanical, photocopying, recording or otherwise, without the prior written permission of the author.

ISBN:     978-1-922644-83-1 (Paperback)

 A catalogue record for this book is available from the National Library of Australia

Cover Design: Ocean Reeve Publishing
Design and Typeset: Ocean Reeve Publishing
Printed in Australia by Clark & Mackay Printers and Ocean Reeve Publishing

Published by Bill Peterson and Genesis Publishing
a self-publishing imprint of Ocean Reeve Publishing
www.oceanreevepublishing.com

To the most remarkable woman I have ever known: my mother.

# Contents

Prologue: The Diary . . . . . . . . . . . . . . . . . . . . . . . . . . . . . vii

Chapter 1: A Childhood During the War . . . . . . . . . . . . . . . . . 1
Chapter 2: Finding My Voice . . . . . . . . . . . . . . . . . . . . . . . 19
Chapter 3: Out of Home . . . . . . . . . . . . . . . . . . . . . . . . . 31
Chapter 4: Life on *Cirrus* . . . . . . . . . . . . . . . . . . . . . . . . 37
Chapter 5: Great Southern Land . . . . . . . . . . . . . . . . . . . . 45
Chapter 6: Across the Country . . . . . . . . . . . . . . . . . . . . . 53
Chapter 7: Life on the Land . . . . . . . . . . . . . . . . . . . . . . . 61
Chapter 8: The Australian Dream . . . . . . . . . . . . . . . . . . . 81
Chapter 9: Living on the Road . . . . . . . . . . . . . . . . . . . . . 95
Chapter 10: My Gold Rush . . . . . . . . . . . . . . . . . . . . . . . 119
Chapter 11: A Mighty Fall . . . . . . . . . . . . . . . . . . . . . . . 133
Chapter 12: The Top End . . . . . . . . . . . . . . . . . . . . . . . . 141
Chapter 13: Back to the Homeland . . . . . . . . . . . . . . . . . . 151
Chapter 14: Paving a New Path . . . . . . . . . . . . . . . . . . . . 159
Chapter 15: A Change of Pace . . . . . . . . . . . . . . . . . . . . . 169

PROLOGUE

# The Diary

My mother was born Aida Bergqvist. On my last visit to Sweden in 2013, I read her diary. I was in my late seventies at the time, and finally understanding what she went through as a child and a young woman brought me to tears. I also understood that one part of her make-up that made it possible for her to survive such incredible hardship was her Christian faith. She was the only family member who was a true believer, and she was very loved and respected as a human being.

Her notes covered her early childhood, and all the hardship endured. Children were the victims of unbelievably hard circumstances, especially if you were a girl. There were many examples of having to simply put up with 'whatever was dished out'. The Spanish flu hit her and two of her siblings in 1918 and, though many people died around them, they survived.

However, after a long and serious time in bed, they could not walk and had to move around on all fours when they got up. When they started school many kilometres away, they had to get there by foot in the winter through very deep snow in the freezing cold. Like most kids living in the region during their school holidays, they were hired by farmers to weed root vegetables grown for the animals, working from seven in the morning to seven in the evening.

Being so poor, they would creep along the ground with bare legs and no shoes. The pay was one and a half Swedish krona per day, about twenty cents in today's market, and on many days, nothing but pigswill to eat. When Mum turned fourteen years old, she got a job as a maid with a very kind family not far from the farm where I grew up. The work was hard; she would be up at four o'clock every morning, hand milk twelve cows, and then work in the fields with the men until evening. The cows then had to be milked again, and the calves and pigs fed. For all that slavery, she received $2.50 per month in today's money. With that, she bought herself a coat—the first one she'd ever owned. She wrote in her diary about the absolute joy of having a personal possession.

Not only did the servants have it tough in those days, but many farmers also found it hard to exist. The farmer she worked for, whose son I attended school with, killed himself. He was found not far from our farm. There wasn't much sentimentality then; the local policeman came to our house and asked for hot water to clean the razor he'd used to suicide before he took it back to the man's family to have it identified.

However, my mother's wage was completely outrageous, especially since she'd been working there for years and loved the family. She got a job with a gardener, Dahlberg, in 1929, a job she loved and would have kept her very busy. There was a big shed on the property, and the whole roof was covered with glass to let the sunlight in, and it was fully heated in winter. She earned the astronomical wage of $4.00 per month and was allowed every second Sunday off.

It was the first time in her life she'd had a whole day free to herself. She was now seventeen years of age. Entertainment for young people back then consisted of getting together at a crossroad somewhere to play music together. Everyone had a mouth organ in those days and sometimes an accordion. To me, it was as if Mum didn't have a childhood, and it makes it easier to understand Mum's unwanted pregnancy to a man who promised her everything.

She was also born with a misshapen face—a deformed left upper jaw—and one side of her face was covered in a purple and red birthmark. Any human being with these afflictions would have been extremely vulnerable to someone offering them love and affection. She worked at different jobs until late in the pregnancy, in 1932, when she moved home to her parents to give birth to my half-brother Nenne.

The stigma she suffered as an unmarried mother was immense, but it was a life she had chosen. The father of her child offered to marry her, but on a visit to his home, the treatment she received was horrific. She decided that she would never expose such evilness to her son and decided to bring her child up alone—what a courageous decision. Nenne was born and looked after by his grandparents while Mum worked to provide for him. She worked for Dahlberg until 1935, with all the money she earned going to her parents for taking good care of her son, whom she loved more than anything on this earth.

Mum worked here and there, sometimes as a cook for the Stackelbergs, who owned a big estate called Stensnas, and at an old people's home until 1936, when she met my Dad, David. He had bought a small farm, named Dundret, in the southern part of Sweden, and was looking for a housekeeper. He turned up earlier than had been agreed to collect her, and Mum didn't even have time to eat her dinner. This was typical behaviour towards women in those days. No consultation was needed, and the women just had to be ready to jump when the men said so.

Dad had a brother helping him at the time, and they both wanted something to eat; all Mum found in the larder was some old pieces of bread and a couple of eggs. Since the main purpose of a woman in those days was to feed the man and bear his children, there was nothing for Mum to eat until after she'd milked the cows that evening and could finally help herself to a glass of milk.

The unbelievable hardship on the farm would have been a great factor in the changed relationship between Dad and his housekeeper; sleeping in the same bed to avoid the terrible cold was unavoidable. The consequences were predictable.

I came along on 21 August 1937, and Sven-Olof (Olle) on 22 June 1939. After a long wait, Mum was united with her son for good when her father brought him to Dundret.

The steely determination Mum showed all her life enabled her to survive those terrible war years, especially when my Dad was absent due to military duties. Mum carried on running the farm single-handed, never complaining, and was loved by everybody. We had an elderly widow living next door, Anna Pettersson, who helped Mum a lot. Everything had to be done by hand, and at the beginning of the war, I was too young to be useful.

Self-examination and reflection are not something I had given much time and credence to in my younger years. Since past mistakes cannot be rectified, I found it a meaningless exercise in self-punishment, with the only likely reward being a depressed mind.

But turning the pages of Mum's diary put me in a state of contemplation about my life. I have been through a lot: from growing up in wartime Sweden to a brief military life and emigrating to the other side of the world—Australia. It is here I found a true home and kindred spirits, throwing myself into farming, mining and any other odd jobs that came my way.

Now in my late seventies, I have found the courage to put my life into words. I sincerely hope the people whose happiness I, in so many ways, may have detracted from can find it in their hearts to forgive. My wish is that my younger siblings, who missed out on the harsh reality of our family's early life, will get a chance to read my book and perhaps understand my mindset, which was formed during those early years.

CHAPTER 1

# A Childhood During the War

My story begins as a little boy growing up on a small farm in Sweden during World War II, with very little to eat, battling to keep warm, and with very little to wear. It wasn't much of a childhood, but it was the only one I had. My experience was far from unique—most kids were in the same situation during the war. Sweden was neutral, but that counted for little when desperately needed food supplies arrived from abroad. The Germans mined the Atlantic Ocean, so very little shipping got through, even the local fishing industry was restricted, and we were going hungry quite often.

My younger half-brother Nenne had a miserable childhood. He contracted a severe illness—some sort of protein poisoning. As a side effect, a rare kind of rheumatic fever made him bedridden for long periods. Because of this, he missed a lot of schooling, and his marks suffered. We went to the same school. Despite the age gap, Nenne was taught by the same teacher as me, in the same room, but I can't remember us ever going to school together as he spent so much of the school year at home.

Nenne told me that one year he was bedridden for seven long months. Just imagine the hardship for Mum; he couldn't walk anywhere, and the toilet was outside, so Mum would've managed his toilet needs along with everything else she had to juggle daily. There is no doubt Mum was the most affected in our family. I know she missed meals at times to make sure her kids had enough to eat; such was the depth of her love for us.

A 'meal' would be a bowl of dry old bread soaked in surrogate coffee in the tougher times. This would be made from roasted acorns and was the least evil tasting of several concoctions, including barley, peas, and other substances. We would often have a concoction like that for lunch, which wasn't much to satisfy hungry kids and certainly not enough for a growing body. This kind of brew was called *ersatz*, which means 'serving as a substitute'. The definition didn't mean squat for me at the time. All I knew was it was not made for culinary enjoyment. It was, however, a great excuse to sit down for five minutes and chat.

In the winter of 1943, the height of World War II, Dad was called up to the army and went to the Finnish border to ensure the Russian armed forces were not getting into Norway through the northern border between Sweden, Norway, and Finland. According to Dad, this was quite a laugh as the only way to the border was cross country on skis. The farm boys kept falling over due to their lack of experience with such equipment, and this could have been a severe disadvantage if they had seen combat in this area. Dad told me that when you get snow stuck in the barrels of your gun, it acts the same way as if you plug it up: the barrels will, more likely than not, blow up. When hunting in the winter, it was standard practice to carry the gun upside down, thus stopping the snow from falling into the barrel when running in the forest and dislodging it from overhanging branches. That

## Chapter 1: A Childhood During the War

was quite different from walking behind the horses on the farm, but my father adapted and overcame like all the other soldiers.

This terribly cold winter saw another addition to our family, my oldest sister Sylvia. She was born at home on 25 November 1942. Dad happened to be home during her birth. The midwife sent Dad and us two boys to the cowshed, out of harm's way and warm enough to survive while the birth took place. The midwife called us back to the house when it was all over.

As we got to the house, I remember the large slush bucket used during the night for our toilet needs had red stains all over it. I went over to investigate since that bucket was always kept inside during those frigid cold days; however, I was told by Dad to leave it alone. I got close enough to see that it was full of the same stuff that the cows used to leave behind them after calving. I knew then that we had a baby sibling.

Imagine the hardship endured by Mum, right up to giving birth, and right back into the hard manual work again after a day or two. When Dad was not home, my eldest brother Nenne had to babysit Sylvia. When Mum needed Nenne and me to help in the cowshed, my younger brother Ollie took over babysitting; a huge responsibility for a three-year-old. We all grew up very fast, and between hard work and some respite when nightfall came, that was the extent of our childhood. Sylvia was the first born of four girls. Clearry came next in 1946, followed by Lillian in 1951 and Kerstin in 1953.

Mum tended to running the farm while Dad was away, and apart from an occasional hand from her brothers and an older woman who was our closest neighbour, she did it single-handed; remember, this was a full-time job when Dad was home. No man could have managed what Mum did since she worked twice the hours as Dad. Menfolk would start working in the fields in the morning, and the women were required to be ready to leave with them. None of the small farms could afford hired help.

Even when Dad was home, life was hard for Mum. When meal break time came along, Mum would rush in to get the meal ready while Dad got the horses unhitched, watered, and fed. After the meal break was over, Mum would be expected to have washed up and ready to leave when Dad was. After the evening meal, she'd be mending or making clothes; she knitted all our socks and sometimes jumpers. Some nights when I came downstairs for a glass of water, she'd still be knitting away.

Yes, I'm sure no man would've managed. We had two horses, half a dozen cows, and the same number of pigs. All the animals had to be fed and mucked out twice a day, the cows had to be milked by hand, and the water had to be carted from the spring. To do this, Mum had to harness a horse to a small wagon with a drum holding maybe 400 litres. It was hand-filled using a bucket and had a tap at the bottom to drain the water back at the stable.

Mum's diary entries during this year opened my eyes to the extent of how hard-going it was for her. The details of her struggle with the elements of that horrible winter continued. She had to cart water from the spring, which was covered with snow most of the time. It was a dangerous task since the spring was quite deep and had no surrounding wall to define its perimeter. The tap in the drum was not much help because, unless it were empty, it would freeze up.

We didn't miss Dad too much while he was in the army. He was a hard man, and circumstances did not allow any time for sentimental family life. It is very hard to show any respect for a man who whipped his kids and horses. Mum never had to use such violence; a tearful look would hurt more than Dad's whip. Having said this, with Olle and me pretty close in age

## Chapter 1: A Childhood During the War

and spirit, we would have been a handful for anybody. Also, the daily worries about food and having enough firewood to keep warm in the winter, sometimes the supply of wood ran out, and Dad would cut up some of the wooden fences around the place. Unless you have been living through such terrible hardship, it is hard to understand

The stick was very much in use in our home, and the carrot, in his mind, was something you fed to rabbits. An old Swedish saying of the times was: 'If you see a young boy loitering, treat him as you would a puppy; if he hasn't done something wrong already, he sure as hell is planning some! Kick him up the arse to keep him on the right track.' Most of the time, the saying was probably right. But, having kids of my own, however little I had to do with their upbringing, has enforced my opinion that physical enforcement achieves little.

I was five, and Olle was three when Dad was called off to war, and I remember enormous numbers of aeroplanes heading for Germany soaring across the sky on cloudless days from our farm, which could be heard a long time before they came into sight. Huge numbers of them could also be seen after the war, flying supplies into Berlin. The city was divided up after the war finished, with no access to the western zone except by air.

The winter of 1943 was bitterly cold, with temperatures sometimes dropping below -40 °C. My oldest brother and told me that one day it was so cold, he had to turn back halfway to school because he couldn't breathe. I received my first pair of skis as a Christmas gift that year, so I could make my way to school when it resumed. Another time, the cowshed had ice on the inside walls and, for those cows next to the wall, there was a possibility they would get frostbite on their udders if they were facing the wall during the night. Because of this horrid winter, the ground was very deeply frozen and didn't thaw out at the normal time in the spring. This was the first time that we had permafrost—ground that is permanently frozen—in our part of the country. Due to the long winter, the feed that been stored for the animals to last a normal winter ran out.

I remember helping Mum and Nenne strip moss from the ground and break twigs from trees to eke out the dwindling supply of feed. There was also a type of acid that could be used to break down newspapers and cardboard boxes. We would mix some acid with water and soak the papers in the solution to make the slurry digestible, though the nutritional value for the herd would have been next to zero. When spring eventually arrived, it was a long time before there was any grass growing because of the permafrost. The poor animals were walking skeletons by the time they were let out into the pastures, and of course, there was no milk to sell for a long time.

The trouble that year continued. With such a long winter, we didn't have enough time during the summer to grow a decent crop of anything. The planting of the cereal crops occurred very late, and the hay crops were pitiful. It made me realise how hard it must have been for the victims of the war. We were told first hand by refugees who arrived in Sweden later that year; not only did they have the abnormally cold winter to deal with, but nobody had any food to spare for those poor people. If they were caught back in their old country, there was a high possibility they would be sent off to labour camps or killed. The lodgings in those labour camps were pitiful. With hardly anything to eat, nothing but wooden boards to sleep on and often no blankets, a lot of those people froze to death.

Some people in Sweden weren't much better off. Dad had a distant relative with a heap of kids who were sleeping on a dirt

## Chapter 1: A Childhood During the War

floor. One of those brutal winters, Dad carted a big load of straw to them and spread a thick layer of it on the floor inside the house. That made it more liveable, but the ground underneath the straw still had frost on top of it. Our own house had timber planks for flooring, which were very hard to keep clean. Every Christmas, Mum would be down on her knees scrubbing them nearly white before spreading finely-chopped juniper twigs on top. The smell of the juniper spreading through the house is a memory still strong in my mind.

Not only was it cold, but we had the deepest cover of snow on record, and the roads were nearly impossible to keep open. The easiest way to get to school was across the lake, which was also used by trucks once the ice was thick enough. Because of the war, the trucks were running on gas produced by a wood-burning apparatus. This fuel produced a lot less power, making the trucks stall on steep hills. Many times when Dad was home on leave, he would harness the horses to help truck drivers get to their destinations when needing to navigate steep inclines. Once they could use the waterways, it was plain sailing.

Dad came home once in the winter to shovel snow onto the house as high as he could reach to insulate it against the cold. This helped to seal the joints between the logs the house was built with. They were squared by axe, and moss was put between each layer to even out the rough surface. Moss, however, is not spongy like foam rubber, and once it dried out, it lost much of its sealing ability. Shovelling snow against the walls was an old trick and very efficient, but it didn't reach the attic where my brothers and I slept. In the evenings, a glass of water would freeze in no time. Dad would come up to the attic where we slept and put his big sheepskin coat over us in the mornings. It was made of a year old length of wool and very warm. Mum and Dad used it during the night, and it was still warm from their body heat when he draped it over his three sons just before the sun began to rise.

One way to stay alive at night was by several people using the same bed. My brothers and I shared the same bed until Nenne got the job as herdsman next door. We had a new house with central heating by now, but because of the extreme cold and very short days during the winter, we spent most of the time in bed. The only lights we had were kerosine lamps or carbide lights. There was always a shortfall of those commodities, and they were only lit when we had to tend to the animals.

We had a pet hamster that used to sleep next to our heads at night, and we would bring it down with us in the mornings. One day we forgot, and by the time we remembered, he was as stiff as terracotta. It was a terrible way for our pet to go, but I have fond memories of our time with him. This little animal was a lot of fun. All of the women I knew were terrified of rats, and this little fellow looked very much like one, creating plenty of opportunities for jokes. The women in the district used to meet at each other's places to sew and knit every so often. During one such meeting at our place, we smuggled the hamster into the room when all the ladies had settled down. It didn't take long before the first scream. In no time, most of the women were standing on top of their chairs.

\*

Sweden has been criticized for staying neutral during the war; however, many thousands of people were saved by doing so. We had 90,000 children from the Baltic states and Finland in every village throughout Sweden. They were poor, traumatised kids who were scared of their own shadow. Growing up, we had a pet dog who would follow us everywhere, and one day, relatives of ours were visiting and had brought a young Finnish girl with them. We were playing quite happily when the dog came over to join us. She became hysterical, scared completely witless because she wasn't used to dogs, but her nerves were shot to pieces by her war experience.

This girl was one of four siblings who were taken in by several families in our district. Two of her sisters were within walking distance from my family home. The oldest lived on a sweeping estate across the lake from my home, the owner of which was David Pettersson. The estate had a school on it and was where I spent my first three years of schooling. The teacher's name was Astrid Ryden-Larson; she was teaching grades one to seven. Her brother-in-law, Paul Larson, was leasing the big property next door. The class sizes were small in those days, and she would've known every pupil's educational standard.

Riitta Lundeqvist, a daughter of the girl staying with David Pettersson, wrote a book about her mother's experiences during the war. Reading the book, *In My Mother's Footsteps,* which was released in 2009, reaffirmed my belief that kids have no magic way of dealing with trauma, despite the popular opinion that children adjust a lot easier than adults. One of those sisters, whose village bombed had been several times, was terrified of thunder. The noise was reminiscent of aeroplanes coming to drop bombs, so every time she heard thunder, she would hide in the cellar, even as an adult. The youngest one of the sisters was very young when they left Finland for Sweden. Whilst in Sweden, even though she wasn't there for long, she forgot the little bit of mother tongue she had, and when she went back to Finland to visit her parents, she forgot the Swedish language. She was now unable to communicate in either language. This perhaps was brought about through her attempts to block out the horrible things that had happened.

During this terrible winter, something very exciting happened in this little boy's life: a refugee camp was established a couple of hundred metres from our farm. Many refugees came across the Baltic Sea in rowboats, and the men, mainly Estonians, were set to work digging pine stumps out of the ground for tar production. They were paid per cubic metre and worked out that if the pieces of wood were stacked precisely on top of each other, leaving some gaps that extra pieces of wood could have filled if one was pedantic about it, they would reach a metre a lot quicker. However, the camp manager was aware of this practice and carried a large sledgehammer with him when he came to measure their stacks of wood. He'd give the stack a heavy blow sideways, and the carefully stacked wood would shift and miraculously condense. The refugees described it as 'Swedish magic': one cubic metre became half a metre.

The refugees were a sorry sight. The first morning the cook at the camp came down to get some milk and told Dad he could drink a litre of fresh milk in one go. 'You're on!' said Dad. The man drank it all right but was sick straight after.

Another day, the man spotted some old hens a neighbour had given Dad. They were so old they had barnacles growing on their legs; the only thing they were good for was fox bait. You'd kill one and put it out at night in the winter, hoping to lure a fox within shotgun range. Fox skin used to be worth a lot of money in the winter, and farmers used to sit in the cow barn or the hayloft above, if it wasn't too cold, during moonlit nights in the hope of shooting a fox.

Things were so desperate that some men would spend a whole night outside in freezing temperatures attempting to get one. They would cut a square hole in one of the many straw stacks that were built when thrashing the harvest in the paddock. This happened quite a lot before self-propelled harvesters came along. The hole would be just big enough to fit in, just deep enough so only the top of your head would stick out. That way, you would keep warm enough and, if lucky, score a fox.

Coming back to the old hens, the refugee, a cook at the camp, asked Dad, 'Can I buy a chicken?'

'No,' Dad told him. 'They're too old to eat, but I'll give you one.'

The next day, the cook put his arms around Dad in a big hug. 'We had chicken soup!' he said. 'Beautiful chicken soup, thank you. Thank you!'

Dad had tears in his eyes when he related the episode later to Mum, 'Poor bastards,' he said. 'You would've thought the pot would've melted before the chooks were tender enough to eat.'

They were marvellous people who worked very hard to fit in. As children, they would give us piggy-backs, sing in their native language, and dance. In the summer, you could see them walking down the meadows in the evening to the lake to do some fishing. In those days, men wore nightshirts instead of pyjamas, and it looked like a Ku Klux Klan group on the move, minus the hats.

The dynamite supplied to them to blast the stumps out of the ground was now used for fishing. A mix of bran and lard was rolled into small balls that they would put in their mouth, swim out into the lake, and spit out. The small fish would come in to feed on this mix, followed by the pikes and the perches. As soon as the men could see the big fish feeding, they would put a stick of dynamite—with a lit fuse attached—in their mouth, swim out to where the fish were feeding and drop the charge. As soon as the charge went off, everyone swam out to collect the stunned fish. There were several rowing boats tied up nearby—every landholder had one—but those people never used or even 'borrowed' one, proudly swimming out instead.

This was not the way the explosives were supposed to be used, but the camp manager, who was Swedish, shut his eyes to this practice. These men were trusted with the explosives, which were freely available to them, and were free to move around at will.

There is only one memory I have of one of the refugees causing a little bit of hassle for our family. One day, Dad was going to the mill to get some grain crushed for the animals but couldn't find enough bags. 'I know what happened to them,' he said. 'There are still some at the camp. I'll go and get them.'

Like all nosy little boys, I tagged along. The cook who was in charge of the bags couldn't find them and the camp manager became quite annoyed. 'They got to be somewhere unless you've eaten them,' he said.

The cook became most upset, 'I no eat bags,' he said in broken Swedish, but we found them. The cook had used them as extra padding under his mattress.

Along with everything else that made life growing up on the farm hard was the constant shortage of money. We could never go to the cinema or any other kind of entertainment. There were plenty of outdoor events with artists from all over the world touring the country during the summers, but since nothing came free of charge, we were stuck on the farm. An incident that made me realise the hopeless position of a poor farmer like Dad was the day when the tax department sent someone to take our only horse, Frej, as payment for outstanding taxes. The mother of that horse had died of old age a couple of years earlier. Dad, not having the means to replace her, used to borrow a horse from one

## Chapter 1: A Childhood During the War

of the neighbours when he needed two. How he could owe any taxes beats me; he never earned any money.

Dad was lucky not to have lost Frej years earlier when he got into a fight with a big elk bull. It was mating time, and the bulls get very aggressive. We came out in the morning to find the paddock all dug up from the fight. Frej had been hit in the chest by the elk, who will fight with their feet as well as their very sharp antlers. There was only a big bruise on the chest, but the hindquarters were a mess. Frej, having tried to kick the elk, was gored by it, and a big chunk of the muscle on one side was missing. It was too big a hole to stitch up; we had to put sulphur powder on it several times a day to stop it from going off. It also had a fly repellent in it to keep the flies away.

Frej spent all summer in the yard next to the house with such an injury while the wound healed. He eventually recovered, but the skin on that hindquarter was very tight when he was working. After being taken from our farm, he was bought by a livestock agent supplying horses for the timber industry in the north of the country. Because of his character, Frej would never give up on anything; I never ceased to wonder about the size of the logs this beautiful animal would shift. Being sold to the timber industry would undoubtedly have meant a life of hard work and abuse by strangers, to whom he was just another horse.

It was like losing a sibling. I sat up in the attic and cried my heart out, promising myself that I would never be in a situation like that. I was just a kid, and most of my time was filled with very hard work. Losing Frej was another nail in the coffin. All that I could see in front of me was more misery, and this was probably one part that made up my mind later in life to emigrate. All of these disappointments so early in life made me grow up a hard man.

When the war ended in September 1945, the camp was closed shortly after, and the refugees went home. However, most of them came back every summer to visit the area and the people who had given them a safe haven in their hours of need. Years later, their children would come as well.

*

My sister Clearry, when she was older, married an Estonian refugee named Wello Ruisla, who had come over to Sweden as a five-year-old after the Russians had bombed his home. The Germans had taken anything that could be of use for their war effort before that, like stoves and any other metals. Twenty thousand people were left homeless by the bombing raid and four hundred dead. Wello's father was a doctor providing essential services, and so the family was found another house in order for him to continue his essential service after their former home was bombed. However, the Russians were getting closer, and eventually, the family fled to Sweden on a ship named Juhan. Since there were a lot of refugees arriving in Sweden, a place to settle permanently was hard to find, and the family moved all over the place. They came to a small town called Vastervik in 1948, where Wello's father got a job at St Gertrude's hospital. Wello and Clearry still live in that small town.

After finishing school and a variety of jobs, Wello found a job at a car repair shop. It was while working there that his life took another turn. He realised that he might have been adopted, as many children were during the war. When he asked his adoptive father, he was told the truth. Yes, he had been placed in a home as a nine-month-old baby after his mother had died. He had lost his father earlier on and was subsequently adopted by the Ruisla

## Chapter 1: A Childhood During the War

family sometime later. Wello was one of the lucky children from that war. His adoptive parents had given him a good education and a loving home. I met his foster mother on a visit to Sweden many years ago, and she was a very proud, elegant lady.

It took twenty-five years before Wello found his surviving biological siblings. During the years of Russian occupation, it was nearly impossible even to visit Estonia, let alone ask any questions. One of Wello's sisters is still alive and lives in America, I believe.

I left Wello's home an enriched man after every visit: what a truly remarkable human being he is. He also has enormous knowledge about a range of subjects, with a supreme memory for dates and places. We spent many hours discussing historical events and geography. He's still involved with providing support for his country of birth, as some of the people are still very poor. It will take a very long time to recover from the war, maybe generations.

*

One episode which shamed the Swedish government was the suicide of a group of resistance fighters. As we heard on the radio, they had come across the Baltic Sea in rowing boats in the middle of the winter seeking asylum. The Germans, however, wanted them back, and the government meekly gave in. As they were standing on the pier in Stockholm waiting to be picked up, the locals smuggled in razor blades to them. They all cut their wrists and having their hands in the pockets of their greatcoats. Nobody suspected anything had happened until they started falling over. It is difficult to imagine how many people would have been executed by the Nazis if they'd captured those men alive and forced them to divulge the names of other resistance fighters.

Knowing the terror the kids of this war experienced, I find it unacceptable that children are adorned with medals and allowed to participate in military marches. Surely, it must give them the impression that war is something glorious? How wrong! There are only losers. I find it hard to understand that people that had suffered so much during the Second World War could join another one in Vietnam, the only difference being an unbelievable increase in barbarism. My comments about the two wars are based to a great extent on personal experience as a kid growing up in Sweden and having lost friends here in Australia, young men who were conscripted to the Vietnam War, some being killed over there, and others coming back mentally scarred for life.

The people involved in the Vietnam War should travel to those Asian countries that were attacked during that war. Not only Vietnam but the neighbouring nations like Laos were bombed. Laos had millions of cluster bombs dropped on it, is the heaviest bombed country in history, and had their crops sprayed with herbicides like Agent Orange, named so because it was coloured to make it easier for the bombers to see where their previous loads of poison had been dropped.

This poison was banned in most countries in the world since it affected not only vegetation, the breeding cycle of humans as well as animals and was also cancer-forming. There is no doubt that that was the reason it was chosen. Not only was the countryside destroyed, but the population is still suffering from the effects of this evil poison. Deformed babies are born even after all these years, and a large area of Laos' arable land, of which there is very little since the country is so mountainous, can't be used as there is an enormous number of undetonated land mines

## Chapter 1: A Childhood During the War

still in the fields along with a large area affected by Agent Orange.

Not only were those people attacked for no reason, but their suffering also continues for generations to come. The effect of that herbicide was noticed in Sweden in the 1950s when the authorities in charge of power and telephone lines used it to kill the regrowth under the wires. Elks were giving birth to calves with their intestines outside their bodies, extra limbs or limbs missing. The alternative lifestyle people who lived off the land had abnormally high rates of deformed or stillborn babies. The poison was designed to increase the hormonal activity in the plants, with the result that they grew so fast the root system could not keep up. The leaves were many times their normal size, and since the root system was underdeveloped in comparison, the plant would die. They were virtually starved to death.

The Swedish name of this poison was Hormo-Slyr. 'Hormo' for the hormone component and 'Slyr', the Swedish word for regrowth. This had been well documented long before the Vietnam War, which makes the use of it even more horrendous. All the hysteria about chemical weapons in Iraq and now in Syria is no worse than what took place in Vietnam at the hands of the American and Australian troops. In my opinion, the Vietnam War must rate as high as any on the records of war crimes. Even so, you're made welcome wherever you travel in those ravaged countries, as I found out myself.

There was a television program shown here in Australia about the 245T poison (a component of Agent Orange). It was still being used in this country thirty years after it was banned in Sweden. Many people employed by the government to carry out weed control have developed horrible symptoms, and a lot have died as a result of years of spraying weeds without proper protective clothing. As a matter of fact, they were told it was completely harmless and that you could actually swallow some without any harm.

Whistle-blowers have now revealed that government agencies ordered workers to take quantities of unused poison out into isolated areas and bury it. This was done after the workers' GPs started to connect the poison with common ailments amongst the workers. Compensation claims were filed, yet after twenty years, only one person has been paid a paltry sum that might buy him a small car.

This case is very similar to the asbestos cases in Australia, where the people responsible for the wellbeing of their workforce denied any responsibility for wrongdoing. In those cases, most of the affected numbers were dead before any resolution was reached. The irresponsible use of toxic substances by various authorities has been covered in a variety of news media, and I have come across the materials many times over the years. I have thought long and hard about this and believe the government and the law should be ashamed; justice is achieved according to the size of your bank account.

CHAPTER 2

# Finding My Voice

Although there were many tough times during my childhood, I also have many fond memories of farm life and boyhood shenanigans. When Olle and I weren't fighting, we had a lot of fun together. There were no video games or televisions in those days, so we had to find ways of entertaining ourselves. We'd go horse riding where we couldn't be seen, and on one such occasion, the time for bringing the cows home for milking arrived. The horses were in the same paddocks, so we thought we'd use them for rounding up the cows. The horses didn't mind at all, but the cows with udders full of milk were startled by us bearing down on them at full gallop. By the time we got home to the barn, there wasn't much milk left in the udders; a lot had squirted out as we chased them along. After that episode, our backsides were too sore to ride for a while.

As a little boy, I kept pestering Mum to let me have a go at milking, she finally relented, and the feeling of achievement after filling my first bucket is hard to explain. Thinking back, it was probably the beginning of my life-long fascination with 'mammaries'.

Most of the time, Olle and I would be sent to bring the cows home for milking, and towards autumn, it was pretty tough on us. There would be frost some mornings, and we never wore shoes until winter arrived. The way to save your feet from frostbite was to stand in the steaming cow pads or where they had been urinating. Wearing no shoes all through summer made our feet very tough, and the bottom layer would fall off towards the end of the winter. We'd build huts in the forest and go fishing, most of the time without permission since we couldn't swim. Looking back today, I realise that our parents probably knew when we went fishing, but, being short of food all the time, we were grateful for whatever we brought back.

On one such occasion, though, I nearly drowned.

We were fishing whilst standing on a big rock and arguing about space. I pushed my younger brother over to one side, and the cheeky little bugger pushed me right off the rock. The water would've been quite deep, and I can remember going down to the bottom trying desperately to get a hold of the rock. I had no chance, it was too slippery, and I went all the way down. Coming up, Olle had the presence of mind to grab hold of me and help me up. I don't think it was as much out of brotherly love as out of fear over how he would explain my disappearance. He was quite a clever boy in this way.

Another form of entertainment could be found in the savage roosters, of which we had many, that would chase us. They were left to grow to full size when they would be killed and eaten. We got a lot of value out of one particular rooster, who would chase anything that came near him, so of course, we used to tease him to make him chase us. At this stage, Dad had hired an old retired knight to repaint the outbuildings. He was making his own paint, boiling it in an old copper pot. The rooster used to

## Chapter 2: Finding My Voice

follow him closely, with the old man kicking out at it to keep it at bay. Once he got his couple of buckets filled and walked back to where his ladder was, he was easy prey for the rooster. As soon as he started his way up the ladder, the rooster would attack. The old fellow had a moustache that used to twitch as he was pouring out swear words both at the rooster and at us for laughing at his predicament. One day, Dad caught us in the act, ending the merriment very quickly.

One day the rooster was catching up with my terrified brother. He was screaming for me to help him, so I picked up a stone and threw it at the rooster. It was an excellent shot, and I hit him in the head, knocking him out. But hell, what should we do now? Dad would become mad as he always did; it didn't take much. We were always taught not to waste food, so we took the rooster into the woodshed, and with Olle holding it steady on the chopping block, the neck in the right spot, I used the axe to chop his head off. Now came the hard part: how to justify this barbaric act. Mum was softer than Dad, so we began with her, pleading if we could have a rooster for dinner. 'Not today,' she said. 'We'll ask Dad when he gets home to kill one, and we can have it tomorrow.'

We moved to the next strategy, telling her how we were just playing, throwing stones at an old tin when the rooster accidentally got in the way and was killed. She seemed happy with this explanation, but her biggest worry was that by the time Dad got home, the rooster would have gone off. When you kill an animal, you have to bleed it, or it will not stay fresh for long. 'Don't worry, Mum,' I said. 'We cut the head off it.'

'Oh my, good!' she exclaimed. 'You know you're not allowed to use the axe. You better pray Dad is in a good mood when he finds out.'

As it turned out, Dad was very impressed by his two preschool boys. 'Not bad,' he said, 'but don't make a habit of it!'

Not being allowed to touch the axe had followed an incident when, acting like two little pests, my brother and I had been trying to cut granite with it. When Dad found out, he didn't give us a whipping but told us to turn the big whetstone used to sharpen everything. It was hard going, and we soon developed blisters on our hands. When we tried to slow down, we were told that if we stopped before the axe was sharp, we would get a hiding we'd never forget. It took a long time for the blisters to heal, but the axe was never used as a stone mason's tool again.

There wasn't time for much play, however. We were trusted to take the cows to a pasture, a kilometre or so from our farm. There was no fencing around this pasture, and the cows would cross the public road frequently while grazing; our job was to make sure they were not hit by passing traffic. Mum would pack us some sandwiches for lunch; they were long days. We used to ride the cows while they were grazing, to and from the pasture. I'm sure the neighbour thought we were an odd mob; nobody else would've dreamed of riding a cow.

Our 'odd mob' regularly increased in size by Mum's three brothers, Yngve, Evert and Sture, who spent a lot of time on the farm fishing, hunting, and chasing the girls next door. Thanks to them, we had something to eat most of the time, and they were our main source of Christmas gifts. The youngest one, Sture, worked for the road maintenance authority, and whenever I was walking to school and met the truck that he was on, there was always a coin or a lolly of some sort thrown on the ground behind it for me.

My uncles Evert and Sture would put traps in the lake to catch pikes and perch, which were a delicacy, but they also caught many small baitfish that were gutted and had a wire put through the eyes and hung in rows in the attic for drying. The smell was pretty evil, but they were a good source of protein. Mum made a type of peppery sauce that took your mind off the smell, but even today, seventy years later, I still find the smell of fish soup hard to take, even though I like it.

Even though we were going hungry at times, the fear poor people had for the law was such that most would starve rather than shoot a wild animal out of season. I remember one of my uncles, Yngve, shooting a big woodcock out of season. This was an illegal act, and he was terrified the local police would find out about it, so he crept through the bushes to get it home. It weighed over seven kilograms and fed us for some time.

My uncles contributed a lot to the lighter side of life, always playing tricks on everyone. I remember one day when Mum was coming into the house, having collected the eggs. There were several of them, some were quite small and speckled, and she was worried something was wrong with the chooks. My uncles were having coffee in the kitchen. They suggested quite seriously that perhaps the chooks had the measles. In actual fact, they'd been on the lake fishing that morning and found some birds nest. They were Grebe nests, and like most fishermen, they collected the eggs to stop them from breeding as they are very aggressive and chase smaller birds like ducks away. Grebes are inedible, so nobody cared much about them, and with their spotted eggs, my uncles couldn't resist playing a joke on Mum. She realised she'd been conned and laughed as must as the rest of us.

Many years later, Mum told me an amusing story about my uncles chasing after the girls' next door. They were the daughters of the herdsman on the big estate, and because of the climate, most houses had only a kitchen and a living room where everyone slept together to keep warm in the winter. Two of my uncles challenged their older brother to get into the room one night to 'get lucky' with one of the girls without waking anybody else. He was up to the challenge.

It was summertime, and my uncle tapped the windowpane softly. 'It's not locked,' came a soft whisper. 'Come in, but take care not to step on anyone.'

Yngve slid over the windowsill and crept along the wall, getting whispers to keep him going in the right direction, when all of a sudden, a hand grabbed him and pulled him down onto the floor. *Ha!* he thought, *How easy was that? Wait until I tell the others. They'll be green with envy.*

However, as Yngve was getting into his strides (or should that be getting out of them), he got hold of a little stump of an arm with only a few fingers attached. It was the mother of the girls. She'd been born with the stump; she must have thought all her Christmases had come at once. According to Mum, what happened next was that Yngve jumped off the floor and sailed out the window without touching anything. The idea of a perfect vertical take-off and flight had been born. The English used the idea successfully many years later when they built the Harrier Jet Fighter, the first aeroplane to operate without a runway for take-off or landing. Meanwhile, my uncle's contribution to aviation history has been completely ignored!

There wasn't much to laugh about in those days, but whenever my maternal granddad Axel or my uncles were visiting, there was plenty of it. As a matter of fact, without them, our lives would've been pretty miserable. They would go skiing and fishing with us, and there were many mornings in the summer when a handful of gravel would be chucked at our window in the attic: that was our uncles' way of getting us out of bed. After a couple of hours

## Chapter 2: Finding My Voice

rowing and just as the sun came up, we would get to the fishing ground. After I finished school, they would also take us hunting. Since you had to walk everywhere when hunting, it was nice to have an uncle walking in front of you in the winter when the snow was deep; you could use the holes they made in the snow to step in.

I remember being home from college and helping Dad with a timber cutting contract. One day we'd just finished morning tea, and Dad was feeling for his snuff box. Snuff is a finely ground tobacco and is used by inhaling it through the nose, like cocaine, or putting it inside your bottom lip. As he was feeling around all his pockets, he was getting really worried. He was addicted and used to get quite mad when he ran out of it. I suppose there's not much difference between opium users in the old days or cocaine and heroin.

One day, he ripped the door to the stable right off its hinges because he couldn't get in, and his snuff was inside. It was winter, and we had a lever on the inside to pull it tight. I was spreading some hay out in the manger when he yelled at me to open the door. 'Hang on a minute, I'm nearly finished,' I said. Suddenly, there was a loud noise, and the door flew open. He'd ripped it right off the hinges.

He had a terrible temper and would fly into a rage in a split second. It was not just running out of snuff, though; he had some serious health problems with splitting headaches and depression. Mum said that he had a bad fall as a young man riding his pushbike, knocking himself out for some time. Concussion was not really understood back then; people just got up when they woke up and carried on as normal.

Many people got beaten senseless every Saturday night. It was as normal as going dancing. Men from different villages would congregate at a crossroad somewhere, and like in the animal world, superiority had to be established, usually with your fists. This was where the snuff-box came in handy. Being made of brass, it was deadly as an assault weapon. Maybe his short fuse had something to do with the fall or his participation in the Saturday entertainment. After ripping the stable door off, he spent a fair bit of time repairing it, while in the meantime, letting all the cold in.

I can now relate to his short fuse in some ways. Having very little equipment to farm his property, he was doing everything manually, which of course, is very hard, takes a lot longer, and meant he was half a step behind tasks that had to be done. Always broke, he had no chance of hiring any help, and the only way to get any was to offer his powerful pair of hands in return. This, of course, set him back even further at his own place. Patience was something he could ill afford; everything had to happen at the spur of the moment. I was in the same situation developing my own land many years later when I'd emigrated to Australia. There was never enough money to buy the equipment needed, though. Most of the work was done through incredibly hard, manual work. Knowing the hardship entailed in developing my own farm both physically and mentally, I certainly would never attempt it again. At seventy-plus years of age, I have had both hip joints replaced due to the extremely hard work involved. I'd like to make it very clear: 'social activity' had very little to do with the wear and tear!

Returning to our timber cutting.

'We'll have to knock off early, ' Dad said. 'I can't work without snuff all day.'

We'd driven as far as we could by car but still had to walk a fair way to where we worked, so I wasn't very keen on an early knockoff. 'Just keep going,' I said. 'You're the one who wanted all these logs cut up before it snows on them.'

This was a problem in the winter: the saw miller who had bought the timber had his own man marking the logs where he wanted them cut. When it snowed on them, you had to sweep the logs to find the marks. He grunted something, but after lunch, he refused to get started. 'I can't go on,' he said. 'Let's go home.'

'No way, ' I said. 'There's plenty of daylight left.'

But he wasn't much use, walking about with a vacant look on his face. All of a sudden, his face lit up. 'Look, smoke,' he said. 'I think I know who lives over there, and he uses snuff.'

Of course, smoke could be seen a fair distance away, but off he went, making a deep trench through the snow. When he came back an hour or so later, he was a different man, he would have had some snuff with the man he visited, and he was now visibly relaxed and on a nicotine high. When it started to get dark, I began putting my tools away so that we'd get back to the car before it was too dark.

'What are you doing?' asked Dad. 'Knocking off already? It's still a good half an hour before dark.'

I could do nothing but laugh.

When my schooling finished, I was ready to give Dad a hand. Life was going along just fine, but he was becoming increasingly harder to please, and I was quickly coming to the conclusion that the farm was not big enough for the two of us. I also realised that I had been very naïve, thinking that life on the farm would change much as I got older.

It was around this time that Nenne finally won the approval of my father. Like many people with low literacy standards, Nenne made up for it in practical ways. There was hardly anything he couldn't fix, which in my opinion, really annoyed Dad; he used to call my half-brother some pretty insulting names. A favourite one was 'bloody cuckoo chick'. Nothing was ever to Dad's liking, and there was a lot of physical abuse. However, one thing that has stayed in my mind all these years happened on our neighbour's farm.

The young people in the countryside had formed a club called SLU. This stood for Swedish Country Youths or Svenska *landungdomar*. They performed amateur theatre and organised dances in the summer, which were usually held in some farmer's big barn. They held competitions like tractor driving and all the other different work performed with a tractor. On this particular day, it was ploughing. This was done with a hydraulic three-point linkage at the rear of the tractor, carrying a plough. It was a relatively new concept, and only the very wealthy farmers had them.

My Dad, my brothers, and I were there, and when David Pettersson, the farmer hosting the competition, saw my older brother longing to compete, he asked him if he would like to borrow his tractor and have a go. You bet he did! He'd never operated a rig like this before, but he was very good at anything mechanical and finished up winning second prize. This in itself was very impressive but paled significantly compared with the miracle that happened next.

When the prizes were handed out, the second prize was won by 'my boy!' as Dad told it. My brother had instantly evolved from being a bloody cuckoo chick to 'my boy who got silver'. Talk about hypocrisy being spoken of in such endearing terms. Nenne, my half-brother, grew up to be a well-respected man of many talents. Having been told to shut up most of the time while living at home, he was a man of few words but a lot of knowledge.

## Chapter 2: Finding My Voice

Many years later, Nenne left a well-paid job in town and moved home when our parents were past caring for themselves. This enabled them to stay on the farm for many years and Mum to stay the rest of her life at home, where she died at the age of eighty-nine. This was a sacrifice I could understand, given the special relationship between Mum and her firstborn. At my last visit in 2017, Nenne was moving to a small town himself, having turned eighty and not able to cope out on the farm. I helped him move, and it was a sad day; our last connection with our family home was severed. I have a lot of respect and admiration for my eldest brother and quite a lot of regret that I didn't do more to ease the miserable childhood he had.

Seeing this sort of behaviour from my father towards my brother was what drove an anti-authority ethos in me. I prided myself on treating everyone as an equal. Later in life, my shearers commented on the fact that my place was the only one where they would sit down and have a glass of Port and a cigar with the boss after the shearing finished. I know that my children have inherited this desire for equality as well, which pleases me no end. I used to employ younger people whenever I could. This was in no small way due to how I'd been brought up. Even though I've been critical about the harsh treatment from Dad, the work ethic instilled in me by him has stood me in good stead. This is the problem with today's society: no work ethic equals little pride and consideration for other people. The best workers I've had were never men in the prime of their life. Instead, they were often those with a point to prove: women, older workers, and even young children

Our conflicting morals brought an end to staying at home and helping Dad. The farm was too small for both our temperaments, but from a purely economic view, I was becoming a drag on the resources. It came up in conversation several times before Dad and I agreed that I could start working for David Pettersson's son, Lennart. He was farming in Hallingeberg, in another district some distance away. Nenne was now working as a herdsman on the big estate next door. This was the very same job the man with the daughters used to do. Olle, my younger brother, would now take on the role of helping Dad around the family farm. This was one of the most exciting days in my life, and I found the night very long before my boss to be picked me up in the morning.

CHAPTER 3

# Out of Home

This was to be the happiest time of my life. While our farm was pretty isolated with no young people nearby, the new community of Hallingeberg I'd moved into to work at Lennart Pettersson's farm was heaven. We had a community hall a kilometre or so away, and every Thursday, a film was shown. There was also a library, and dances were frequent, with girls galore. I felt like this was the birthplace of free love, and I, having grown up a little shy, became a party animal.

The farm where I was employed belonged to the church, and just over the fence was the home of the priest, who had two daughters and a son. One morning, when I came into the room where we emptied the milk buckets, I was struck with awe by the most beautiful girl I'd ever seen. It was Eva, the eldest of the daughters. She had come down to collect the milk for the priest's household, something that he always used to do. But, she told me later, she'd seen me working in the field and decided to check me out. I was mesmerized. We fell very much in love. I had a motorbike, and we went everywhere. She had very broad-minded parents, and I realise today what truly remarkable people they were. They saw me as a hardworking, honest young man and readily accepted me into their home, even though the busybodies in the village could not accept that a priest's daughter and a poor farmhand were dating. In Australia fifty years ago, you would probably have been shot for a liaison like that! Her parents, however, had nothing to worry about; Eva was a very level-headed girl who would not have done anything to disappoint her parents. She was also the only girl in my life that I never tried to seduce; she meant too much to me.

This heavenly situation came to an end when Eva went to university and I joined the air force in 1957 to complete my national military service. I was lucky enough to get into a special unit and spent a lot of time after my initial training guarding aircraft and installations all over the place. This gave me plenty of opportunities to meet people from all over the world since some of the islands where we held our manoeuvres were very popular with tourists. I'm ashamed to say that it also led me back into the partying life I'd lived before I met Eva. Seeing how quickly I regressed made me realise in no uncertain terms what an impossible future we would have together; we had such different backgrounds and different ways of living.

After a blissful couple of weeks on an island in the Baltic Sea, where I spent most of the time kicking a soccer ball around, and the unit could have as much time off as needed for practice thanks to our sports-mad captain, we got back to a pretty dull life on the mainland. While I was on leave one day, I enrolled at an Agriculture College. The air force then granted me leave for the duration of my studies. The aim of my enrolment at the college was twofold: to further my education and perhaps skip the last two months of my military service. I thought wrong. Not long after my exams, I got a letter from the airbase F3, located about

## Chapter 3: Out of Home

100 km from my family farm, asking me to return to finish my service. This was between recruitment dates, and when I turned up, the sergeant who was my commanding officer during my original training was not impressed. '821 Peterson, ' he said. 'I thought we'd gotten rid of you. What the hell are we going to do with you?'

I had expected this scenario and had taken the step before I went back to the base of ringing Harry Angelof, the boss I'd had after my initial weapon training. I had been employed in a workshop that serviced and built batteries for all the planes and vehicles. He was a civilian, and we had become very good friends. He even invited me to his place one night for a meal. Harry had a very nice wife and a daughter who reminded me of the American actress Kim Novak. If you read this, Mona, I thought you looked fantastic. I asked Harry whether he could contact the officer in charge of the section and ask him if I could spend the two months with him. 'Consider it done,' he replied.

When I told the sergeant about this arrangement, he smiled and said, 'That's the best news I've had all day!'

I went back to Harry Angelof's workshop and sat on my arse for two months. That must have done a lot for Sweden's national security! While I was filling in time at the airbase, I went to Stockholm to inquire about the emigration program the Australian government was promoting, undertaking an interview with an Australian official. There were some forms to fill in and a few week's later I received a letter to say that I had been accepted.

After a lot of thought, I decided to emigrate. The promotion Australia was running in Sweden was very encouraging, promising as many opportunities as America did at the beginning of the nineteenth century when many Swedes took a gamble on a better life in that country. I took stock of my life and realised my future looked less than promising, especially given the wild party life I was currently living. Having gathered no assets of any description, I didn't think I was strong enough to change my ways if I continued in the environment I was in, and hence the decision to emigrate was made.

Some of my plans had worked to some degree. But how would I get to Australia, and where would the money come from to pay for the trip? When you are the district's champion party animal, there's not much in the kitty for travel! After checking the ticket price, I offered the farmer I worked for, Yngve Pettersson, a contract to cut the farm's timber quota for that year. I wound up the chainsaw and got stuck in, working every hour there was. At a local dance some weeks later, a farmer on the other side of the lake asked me if I had a tanker attached to my saw: he had never heard it stop. It was hard work, but once the decision was made to get out of the place, it made no sense to hang around. The women folk on the farm—Ingeborg, the wife of the owner and their daughter, Irma—used to make porridge for my lunch and put it in a thermos, ensuring I had something hot to eat. Some days it got very cold, and at times I worked in temperatures nudging minus twenty. Steel becomes very brittle in temperature like that, and one day my brand new axe broke in half when I tried to cut a tree limb off.

After a couple of months, I'd made enough money to pay for the ticket and started looking for transport. One of the incentives to emigrate to Australia was to stay for a minimum of two years, and the Australian government would pay for two-thirds of the ticket price. As it turned out, several Swedish cargo ships carted fruit and grain from Australia and took paying passengers back on the return trip. The ship I ended up on was very fast, with a top speed of twenty-two knots and a loading capacity of eleven thousand ton. This was perfect: the trip would take a couple of months but included quite a few calls at ports during the journey. Fantastic! A bit of sightseeing for the same price. Despite my plans, it was a worried young man who stepped aboard the Cirrus (like all the ships in that company, it was named after a cloud). The furthest that I'd been away from home before in my life was Stockholm, just 300 kilometres away, during my emigration interview.

CHAPTER 4

# Life on *Cirrus*

If I'd thought I was a playboy in Sweden, where at least we worked during the day, my journey on the *Cirrus* in 1961 showed how tame I had been in the past! Onboard, it was as if my party life was amplified ten-fold. There was constant partying, and the perfect way to describe most days was a 'haze'. The crowd I partied with saw no excuse for not getting up the morning after, but when I finally dragged myself out of bed, I would never get further than the closest deckchair, where I would spend hours on end doing a whole lot of nothing. This turned out to be a lethal mix: white-skinned hungover passengers, deck chairs, the burning hot sun and the sun's reflection off the water led to awful sunburn. During the ceremony at the Equator crossing, I was so burnt I couldn't bend my legs, and I'm sure many skin cancers I've suffered from later in life were initiated on that crossing.

There were sixteen passengers on the ship, including a German family; a newly married English couple; a retired Australian school teacher; an elderly American lady; a Swedish retired farmer, Arvid Bergqvist; a Swedish sailor, Karl-Otto Bjorkstrom;

a Maltese married woman with two little girls; the first mate's wife; and myself. The first mate's wife was a lonely, card-playing addict, and Charlie, the Swedish sailor and I spent a lot of time in her cabin playing cards. The rules were that the loser would supply the drinks. Charlie and I had designed a system that made it nearly impossible to lose, and so spent the best part of a week getting very happy at her expense. However, her husband came in during one of our games one day, and he was not a happy man. 'Get the hell out!' he yelled. 'You've drunk all the grog that I am allotted to entertain guests!'

Being gentlemen, we left and in future played in the entertainment area, though she was still paying for most of the grog.

\*

Crossing the Equatorial line was a significant occasion. Due homage had to be paid to King Neptune; it's a rite of passage that was recognised onboard our ship. The ritual included eating rotten and very spicy food, ingested while being held down by a couple of the King's black painted guards, so there was no escape. You were also painted with a mixture in a horrible colour, which lasted longer than anything British Paints had produced. At the dinner table that evening, some guests voiced their concern about the severity of the ceremony. The captain, Bamse, a nickname meaning 'bear' in Swedish, stood up. 'What a mob of old women,' he said. 'When I went across the first time, people would faint. We would throw them in the swimming pool, and if they didn't come back within a certain time, then we'd go and check on them! If they'd gone blue in the face, we'd pull them out, and on top of that, we'd cut a cross in their hair with a pair of clippers!'

## Chapter 4: Life on Cirrus

Bamse was as bald as a peeled egg, and I, in my drunken state, couldn't help myself. 'What about people with no hair?' I asked. 'You would have to use sticky tape on them.'

In a flash, this giant of a man, the best part of 150 kilograms, got to his feet and headed for my table, grabbing a rhubarb pie the size of a dinner plate off the service trolley along the way. He slapped it down in front of me and said, 'Don't leave the table until you finish that. It should keep you quiet for a while, and if you do leave the table before you finish, I'll put you in chains for the rest of the trip.'

The first mate, he with the card-playing wife, looked across the table at me. 'You may not know,' he said gleefully, 'but on a ship, the captain's got absolute power.'

Coming from a protected background, I was quite worried that I would be held to this and what it would do to my stomach if I attempted to consume this whole pie on my own. But when everyone had left the dining room, Bamse came over to me. 'I'll let you off this time, ' he said, 'but you owe me a duel in the swimming pool tomorrow.'

I knew that I wasn't off the hook. Not only did he look like a polar bear, but he also swam like one, too, while my swimming ability was limited to keeping afloat. The next day, I didn't go anywhere near the swimming pool but remained in the safety of my cabin, catching up on some letter writing.

While leaving the table the night of the pie incident, we had been informed that there would be free after-dinner drinks served in the entertainment area: this we would not miss. Having already consumed enough drinks to kill off anything that resembled common sense, Charlie and I got into an argument as to who could handle their grog the best. It could not be decided at the table, so we decided to race each other to the top of the ship's crane: that would sort the boys from the men.

The crane had ladder rungs around it, which made it easy to climb. If we thought the ship was rolling at deck level, it was nothing compared to ten metres above the deck. We must have been hanging out over the water at times, but that didn't worry us at all since it was pitch black. I'm not a religious person, but something protected me from falling overboard that night. After our race, Charlie disappeared, and as it was now well after midnight, I decided to go to bed. As I headed towards my cabin, I ran into Elly, the card-playing blonde and Lena, the woman with the two little girls. They got on each side of me and told me they were taking me back to my cabin. *This is my night,* I thought. Not only had I beaten Charlie, but here was I taking two beautiful women back to my cabin, something I had spent weeks trying to accomplish without any luck. The last thing I remember, however, was opening the cabin door!

The next day, just before lunch, there was a knock on the door. 'Come in,' I said.

There stood Charlie, his light grey suit wrinkled and still covered in soot and grease from our climb the night before. 'What a night, ' he said. 'I crashed out before I got undressed. How about you?'

'Charlie,' I said, 'you have lost the competition as the toughest guy on this ship. I hung my clothes up, as I have done since the age of four, you know, and I brought Lena and Elly back to my cabin.'

He went to my wardrobe to check my suit was indeed hung and agreed that I was the hardest man he had ever met. It was nearly lunchtime, so I suggested that we'd meet in the dining room. He turned a funny colour and left.

Charlie never made it to lunch, but the two ladies who had brought me to my cabin the night before were there, though they

## Chapter 4: Life on Cirrus

didn't say much. At dinner that night, Charlie made an effort to give a speech in English, referring to our competition the night before. 'Bill,' he said, 'is the toughest bloke that I ever met. Not only did he match me in everything, but when I called into his cabin this morning, he looked as fresh as ever. I also believe that he is a bit of a lady killer as well!'

I felt eight feet tall! Lena, who I thought was looking at me with affection, turned out to be pitying me instead and spoke up. 'Bill,' she said, 'can you remember Elly and me taking you back to your cabin last night because you were very drunk? Elly and I watched your suicidal antics up that ladder, and we were concerned about your welfare. We undressed you and put you to bed. I hope the clothes were hung up all right; I usually don't put boys your age to bed.'

The thump as I came back to Earth must have rocked the ship. The grin on Charlie's face was unbearable.

*

Choosing a cargo ship as a means of transport to Australia turned out to be a smart decision. Not only did we have private cabins, but we spent a lot of time ashore while the ship was unloading or taking aboard cargo. On one such occasion in the port of Beira in Mozambique, we went to a nightclub. The beauty of the Portuguese-African women was irresistible, and we partied into the early hours of the morning.

When I woke up, I had very little recollection of what had happened the night before. The rest of the party were still asleep, so I got off the mat on the floor where we'd been sleeping and went for a walk. Everywhere I looked, fruit trees were growing, and I realised we were on a plantation. We didn't know that the night before since it was dark when we arrived, and the girls couldn't tell us. Not much Portuguese was spoken where I'd come from, and, I guess, not much Swedish was spoken in Mozambique. All communication we had with them was through sign language and touch. As I stood there wondering where the hell we were, a young man came walking towards me. Unable to speak the local language, I hunched down in front of him, drew a picture of a ship in the sand, pointed at myself, and drew an arrow pointing to the ship. He gave me a big grin, his face full of blindingly white teeth, sat down next to me and drew a picture of a bus in the sand. He then drew an arrow leading to where we were standing and another one connecting it to the ship. We understood each other: we could get back to the ship by bus.

By now, Charlie had woken up and was walking down the track to where we were. The two girls we'd spent the night with were with him. We had some fruit for breakfast, and shortly after, a bus arrived. We got on, and after what seemed like a long journey, we arrived at the port, and thank God, the one with our ship in it. We'd taken the girls back to the plantation the night before in a taxi and, had it been back in Sweden, we would still be paying the fare off.

The tender that ferried the passengers back and forth between ship and port at low tide was skippered by the first mate. He was still smarting about the grog his wife had wasted on us. He was also clearly disapproving of our interaction with the locals, and he put his nose in the air and said in a quite loud voice: 'There is a peculiar smell around here.' His opinion didn't bother us very much, but given the copious amount of alcohol consumed during our card games, he should have considered himself lucky that there was not a German whiff in the air.

## Chapter 4: Life on Cirrus

Back on board, we had a well-needed shower, a proper breakfast, and after a few hours' sleep, decided to hop on a bus and see a bit of the countryside. The cost of transport was very cheap and, as it happened, we ended up at the same plantation where we'd spent the previous night. In retrospect, it was probably the only road with public transport.

The people were very friendly, and we were invited to play soccer with a group of kids. Soon the whole village was involved. I supposed it was as much of a novelty for them as it was for us. The ball was an animal stomach stuffed with very fine, dry grass, but it worked surprisingly well. As we were getting ready for the return trip to the ship, a young boy sold us a big bunch of bananas for a ridiculously low price and insisted on carrying it onto the bus. It had been a memorable day, and I'd taken plenty of photos.

Mozambique was not the first time we'd been clubbing while ashore. We also ventured into Cape Town, South Africa. We visited some of the highest class nightclubs in the world. Apartheid was very much evident in South Africa at the time and put a bit of a dampener on the nightlife. We also visited the wine-growing areas around Table Mountain. Fifty years later, I'm still drinking wine from that area; it is very good quality and well-priced. Cape Town is also where I first came across the Holden motorcar. I was told it was made in Australia, which confounded me as it looked very much like a Chevrolet made in America. As it turned out, they were both backed by General Motors.

Back on board, I helped out Lena by babysitting her two little girls a couple of times so that she could go ashore without having to worry about taking them along. I did this; I'm ashamed to say, not only because I loved those kids, but because I thought it would improve my chances with their mum. However, there was no chance: she was the most loyal wife anyone could wish for and a pleasure to have for company on that long journey. I had a lot of great times with the children, but I came back to my cabin one day and found the little girls playing, something they'd done many times before, only this time, they'd found my camera. They'd rolled out all of the film on the floor, and not one photo of my trip to that point could be saved.

CHAPTER 5

# Great Southern Land

The first time we spotted Australia was along the coast of South Australia in June 1961. There were lots of fires burning, which were easily spotted at night. It looked like the whole countryside was alight. We were told it was settlers clearing the land. Little did we know that we would one day be spending a lot of time doing just that ourselves in a bid to make a new life. The day was approaching when we would leave the *Cirrus*, and it was a bittersweet milestone.

We arrived in Melbourne on a miserable winter's day. We were told we would be met by emigration officials who would inform us about what would happen next. It was a very worrying situation; we'd become a family of sorts on that long trip, and most of the English speaking passengers were met by friends and relatives at the dock. The only passengers who didn't know what was to become of them were Charlie, the Kroc family, and me. I worried that if we were split up and sent to God-knows-where with our limited abilities to speak English, it would be a disaster. Emigration officials spoke English only, so there was no help there. They produced stick-on labels with an address on it—our destinations—and stuck that on us. We felt like Christmas parcels being sent somewhere, but upon comparing notes, we found we were all going to Bonegilla, a large camp for emigrants around 300 kilometres northeast of Melbourne. Great relief was felt by us all.

Bonegilla was a former army base, which was now a centre for emigrants. There were about 5,000 people there when we arrived. They were from all over the world, and the base was a melting pot with many different languages spoken. I was astonished to find out that some people had been there for more than three years, a very different story from the one told to me by the Australian emigration official in Stockholm. According to him, there was zero unemployment in Australia.

The housing was pretty basic, with just one 1,000-watt heater in each quarter, which held two beds. We would put them on the floor with the heater coil facing upwards and use them for toasting bread, or, as happened at our Swedish midsummer celebration, we put a metal tray from the kitchen on them and used them for grilling steaks. This particular evening turned into a pretty wild party, with a guy from Stockholm being sick on my bed. I threw him out, washed the blanket the next day, and left it on the clothesline while we went for lunch. I learned a lesson from this because when we returned, it was gone. From that time on, I never took my eyes off anything that was mine. I managed to tell the Camp Superintendent that the blanket been stolen, and luckily he believed me, or I would have had to pay for it.

The barracks had no insulation. As army barracks, they were not known for their luxury. We were given five woollen blankets each, and while we didn't freeze, the water in the puddles outside was frozen solid on most mornings. We couldn't complain: we were given three meals a day with some choices, a film was shown once a week, and we had English lessons daily. The families who had been there for half a year or more got a pair of free shoes for each of their kids. Some of the true Catholic believers with half a dozen kids or more would have been a lot better off staying in the camp indefinitely.

A shapely redhead was teaching us to sing in English, who was married to the Camp Superintendent and a migrant herself from Finland. She told us about her first experience of Australia when she was newly engaged and visiting her fiancé's home in Queensland for the first time. During the night, she wanted a drink of water. Not wanting to disturb anybody, she went to the kitchen without turning the light on. She was doing all right until she stepped on something cold and wriggly. Hearing her screams, her fiancé came running and turned the lights on. Across the kitchen and stretching into the next room was a large python snake. 'He's a beauty, isn't he?' said her fiancé. 'The biggest in the district, about twenty feet long. Sorry, I forgot to tell you about him last night. Don't worry about him, though; he's pretty harmless and quite tame!'

This was a very casual attitude indeed. Those snakes can swallow fully-grown geese, and there was an article in the paper a couple of years ago about a boy who was nearly eaten. His parents heard a noise from his room one night and, when they went to investigate, found their son in the snake's mouth, only millimetres before his mouth would've been covered. If they hadn't heard the noise, he would've been missing in the morning. It's not so easy to tell what a snake that size has eaten. When they eat big prey, they compress the body into a much smaller diameter to be able to swallow it. I watched one eating a possum one day; as soon as he got the head of the possum into his mouth, he compressed the body to the same thickness, almost like making sausage.

Coming back to our English lessons at the camp. We were singing the song 'How Much Is That Doggie In The Window?' and after the first line, Charlie and I yelled, 'Woof woof!' to lighten the atmosphere. The next time that line came around, the place sounded like a dog kennel.

Camp life became very boring within a week, so Charlie and I decided to take a walk around. We spotted some horses in a paddock during our stroll, and since I love horses, we went over to pat them. As we stood there, a woman called out to us from a cottage some distance away. She was pointing to a shed on the other side of the paddock, and we could just make out something about her husband being over there. Having 5,000-plus foreigners on her doorstep probably made her a bit jumpy. However, we walked over to the shed, which turned out to be a dairy, and met the farmer who was cleaning it out; he'd just finished milking for the day. He seemed friendly enough, so I flexed my biceps and told him in very broken English that I wanted work.

'There's heaps to do on this farm, ' he said, 'but no wages.'

I understood this perfectly, a lot better than he would have understood my English. This was looking pretty good. The fact I wouldn't be paid didn't worry me at all because anything would be better than being cooped up in the camp. 'I help you,' I said.

He looked me straight in the eye, 'No money remember, but I'll feed you. Come tomorrow.'

As soon I'd finished breakfast the next morning, I was off next door to start work for Ron Rapsey. This was an opportunity too good to miss, and we worked hard to clean the paddock up. There was lots of fallen timber, some of which were quite large logs. We also burned dried up carcasses of dairy cows which had drowned during a flood the year before, and some that had died from lack of feed the year before that due to drought. It hit home

## Chapter 5: Great Southern Land

to me how savage and unreliable the climate was in this country. We were stacking the bodies on some fallen dry timber when we got to mid-morning, and Ron called out, 'Come on Bill, smoko time!'

I looked bewildered at him, *What was he talking about? I didn't smoke.* He pulled out a basket from under a bush and proceeded to produce sandwiches with homemade fig jam as filling and poured a milky coloured liquid into a couple of mugs. The sandwiches were delicious, and the drink tasted nothing like anything I'd drank before. 'What's this?' I asked.

'Coffee,' he answered.

'How you make it?' I asked.

'You use piping hot milk and coffee. How do you make it in Sweden?'

'With water,' I said.

'Water?!' He looked horrified: water is used strictly for washing in this country.

Ron was a fantastic man with a very generous and understanding wife. Stella, I think her name was. They had a couple of young boys. I intended to learn as much as possible while working with Ron and then see if I could buy some farmland for myself.

'Not here,' Ron said when I spoke of my intentions. This was River Gum country; it cost too much to develop because the trees were too big. I walked around one, and the circumference was over eleven metres, a diameter of nearly four metres! The only way to get rid of them was to ring bark the trees and burn them once they were dry enough. No machine had been invented that could push them over. Hardwood dries at the rate of 2.5 to 3 centimetres per year, so you'd be too old to be allowed out with matches by the time the trees would burn. Some trees would take close to a hundred years to dry.

This was a hell of a setback. I wasn't very keen on the idea of staggering about at the age of ninety burning half-dried trees. All was not lost, however; Ron had some ideas of his own. 'You want some cheap land for farming?' he asked. 'You're in the wrong state. You're a hard-working young bloke with your whole life in front of you—go to Western Australia. The government is making millions of acres of virgin land available for farming at very cheap prices. It so happens that I have the relevant application forms, and I'll fill them in for you fellas.'

Ron was going to apply himself, but his family talked him out of it, age being one factor. This was truly one very goodhearted and compassionate family.

One day, Ron told me we were going to Wodonga to attend a livestock auction. There would be plenty of dairy cows for sale, and he wanted me to prove my knowledge about dairy farming by picking out a really good one. Afterwards, he bought lunch for the three of us, and his wife had come along as well. 'What would you like to eat?' he asked, having already ordered himself.

'Steak and chips and a couple of eggs, please,' I answered.

A look passed between Ron and Stella, and Ron said in a friendly banter manner: 'He might not know much English, but he sure knows where the expensive food is on the menu!' After the meal, he took us to see a football match. I was horrified! It was the first time I had seen an Australian Rules match and couldn't understand how the players were allowed to virtually practice street fighting on the oval.

I had spent a lot of time playing soccer in Sweden, especially during my time in the air force. In those days, it was not permitted to put your hands on your opponent: you depended entirely on your skill to control the ball and your opponent with your foot. 'This is a man's game,' Ron said. That justified everything, apparently.

## Chapter 5: Great Southern Land

While I was working for Ron, he told me about a land board office in Beechworth, forty-five kilometres southeast of Bonegilla, that handled inquiries about land transactions. We hitched a couple of rides to this place and soon realised that our confidence in conversing with those people was greatly misplaced. When I say that our knowledge of the language was basic, that's exactly what I mean. We'd travelled all that way for nothing, having a lot of questions to ask but unable to make ourselves understood.

Now we were worried about how to get back to the camp. Beechwood is in the high country and gets very cold at night. Luck was still with us, though, as a man was building a house close to the road we were walking along. He was German and happened to live in Bonegilla. 'I'll give you a lift back,' he said, 'but you'll have to wait until I knock off.'

We didn't mind this and spent the afternoon walking in the countryside. It was completely different from Sweden: the vegetation was strangely olive green, very hard, and in places prickly, not the lush colour that we were used to. The trees—Mountain-Ash, we were told—were very tall and straight; they seemed to reach into the clouds. As we were walking along, we disturbed some Kookaburras. We'd only heard their mad laugh on film before, a jungle film, I think, where the Japanese were staging an ambush. We didn't know what it was, and they made us jump out of our skins in the first instance. Coming out on the other side of the forest, we walked into a potato field on a hillside with a stream coming out of the ground. The crop was irrigated by running the water sideways in shallow channels.

We'd been walking around for a few hours, and it was time to get back to our German friend. Having to travel such a distance every day to work on his house, he worked until dark, and we were relieved when he eventually put his tools down and started his utility up. After a short distance, however, he stopped, got out of his vehicle and picked up a garden fork from the back. Close to the road was a paddock of potatoes. 'That's mine,' he said. 'I dig a few bags after work every day; there is a market for them back at the pub.'

There was no permit needed to grow potatoes in Victoria, as there was in Western Australia, and he would leave them in the ground until someone wanted some. The ground froze on the surface in the winter, so there was no concern about insects damaging the potatoes. By the time he finished filling the bags and the hour and a half travelling home, it was bitterly cold and pitch black. That night we went to bed without tea.

After two weeks working for the marvellous Rapsey family, it was time to move on. Despite having told me that there would be no wages at the start, he paid me the going rate and wrote me a glowing reference. It was written with the old type of pen with a nib and real ink. I'm humbled to have arrived in a foreign country not speaking the language and receiving a character reference within a few weeks. I still have it and have used it many times. Ron would, without a doubt, be the most important person we met in our new country.

If I had not got off my arse to look for other possibilities by leaving the camp that particular day, I would never have met Ron. That was my chance of starting in my new country, maybe the only one. The moral of this is clear: don't sit around waiting for an opportunity to find you. Go looking for it.

CHAPTER 6

# Across the Country

Although the land contract had not been finalised, I was always one to get my ducks in a row first. Charlie agreed to join me, applying for virgin land in WA. He finished up work with Ron's brother Mick at the same time as me. Even though nothing was guaranteed or officially settled, we had to get to the other side of this enormous country to be interviewed by the land board before we could be considered suitable for land allocation. We had no money, so we decided to hitchhike to Albany, where the land board would be meeting. We didn't realise the distance ahead of us, being too young and stupid. The only equipment we took with us was a rucksack, no raincoats or tent. The hike to Albany turned out to be three times the length of Sweden! We told the cook at dinner the night before of our plans, and he filled our rucksack to the top with food to help us on the way.

However, the next morning as we tried to leave, there was a hell of an uprising in the camp. Residents, mainly those who had been in the camp for up to three years, began rioting. It is amazing how quickly people become used to better living standards. Many of these men came from countries where they'd been living in quarters above where they kept their animals during winter, and not many years before had been trying to survive World War II.

The rioting men in the Bonegilla camp carried a big log on their shoulders and proceeded to level a lot of the buildings. They wanted work, so it's hard to see the logic of their behaviour. A character reference would've been very helpful, and this behaviour certainly wouldn't help. Who would want to employ a mob of wild-looking men carrying a big log? When we got to the gate, there was a burly policeman on guard, who he told us to go back. 'No,' we said. 'We go to WA.'

He pulled out a metre-long truncheon and roared, 'Get the hell back, or else!'

They were probably worried we were going to bring in reinforcements if we were let out. We had no choice and went back to our quarters. But we were not giving in that easy. We went to see the superintendent. He'd known of our plans and supported us completely, so after trying to work out a way to get us out of the camp, he came with us to the gate. After a lot of arguments, heated at times, he convinced the police to let us out.

*Western Australia, here we come!* We'd printed a sign which read 'WA, PLEASE' which we stuck on the back of the rucksack. This, we thought, would save a lot of time trying to tell any motorist who stopped of our plans.

On the first day, we got several rides. One was with a bloke who was driving a car held together with tie-wire and strings. He was drinking straight from a flagon of wine and was quite happy. He offered us a drink, and we began to feel like we were back on the ship again: he was all over the road and moving us around.

As we came around a bend in the road, a mob of cattle was spread across it, feeding on both sides. We learned later that a

## Chapter 6: Across the Country

farmer would turn his cows onto the road when feed is in short supply. The Aussie's name for it is 'the long paddock'. Our friend never slowed down, he weaved from one side to the other, cursing loudly, but we came out on the other side without hitting a single animal. We had second thoughts about his driving then. We'd thought he was drunk, but when we got as far as he could take us, we realised he had no brakes whatsoever. That's why he was so good at dodging the cows!

He dropped us off at a place called Echuca on the banks of the Murray River. Echuca became the second-largest inland port in Australia by the 1870s. Paddle steamers carried huge loads of wool, produce, livestock, and timber to the coastal ports.

This mode of transport was different from the bullock teams who had to fight terrible terrain to get their loads out—the poor animals. We were sitting on the bank of the river, trying to imagine what it would've been like in those days. I was mending Charlie's pants that he'd ripped getting out of that old car—so he'd be decent when we got another lift.

We picked up a few more rides. The last one towards the end of the day was in a semi-trailer. We jumped on the back since the cab was full with the driver's crew. They had been carting grain, and in those days, everything was in bags and required plenty of manpower to move. It got dark and cold very quickly: this was the middle of winter, and we had no idea how cold it would get inland.

We realised we'd made a big mistake accepting a ride on the back. There were only bars for a headboard on the trailer, the wind was icy cold, and the countryside was beginning to turn white with frost. We couldn't make the driver stop, and he was oblivious to our plight: it was too dark for him to see us. We realised we could freeze to death. There was a rolled-up tarp tied to the headboard, and after a lot of struggle, we managed to unroll some of it and got under it out of the wind. It had been a dangerous operation; the truck was doing about ninety kilometres and had no sides to stop you from falling off. If we had, no one would've noticed. The night seemed to last forever, but just before daybreak, the truck stopped. The driver came over to where we were huddled together. He signed to us to get off and shone a torch at a road sign. It was an intersection and pointed to the left. 'WA,' he said.

We were too bloody cold to care. I thought my body was frozen from the waist down as I had no feeling in my legs. Taking a couple of tentative steps, I realised they still worked. We spotted a bridge in Swan Hill in the early morning light and decided to light a fire under it to warm up. After getting the feeling back in our legs, we fell asleep: we'd been on that truck for twelve hours and travelled nearly a thousand kilometres.

We got another ride as soon as we got back on the road. It stopped at Mildura, a little town in the very north of Victoria. It was a clear day, and I remember thinking it was the cleanest air I'd ever breathed. We were itching like hell: the tarp we'd wrapped ourselves in the night before had been used to cover the load, which were bags of oats. The oat grain has tiny little hairs on it: they stick to your skin, which makes you itch, and we were also getting very hungry. I think the last meal had been while we were stopped at Echuca the day before.

As we walked into town, we saw a little cafe and decided to get something hot to warm us up. We ordered a big pot of tea and tipped all the sugar on the table into it for a bit of energy; we didn't have much money for anything else. The owner was a little old lady, and she came over to our table. 'Toast?' she asked.

'No, no,' we said. 'No money,' and pulled out our pockets.

## Chapter 6: Across the Country

Our English was basic, and we thought if we ordered toast and couldn't pay for it, we could get into trouble. She gave us a searching look and went back behind her counter. It wasn't long before she turned up with a stack of toast; it must have been a whole loaf. We thought she'd misunderstood us and pulled our pockets out again, 'See? No money.'

'No worries,' she said. 'Eat.'

That is a phrase I've heard many times since. 'No worries' is an Australian favourite. When we were just about ready to leave, she came over to our table, got hold of my arm and told me to go with her. Well, I've never been able to say no when a woman asks me to come along with her, so I willingly followed. She took me into the back of the shop where she lived, where she'd drawn a hot bath, and there was a razor on the edge of it.

'You've had a hard time,' she said. 'You get cleaned up, and when you've finished, get your mate in here.'

I understood a fair bit of the language by now and duly fetched Charlie when I'd finished. When we came out of there, I said, with tears in my eyes, 'One thing I know for sure, this boy is not going back to Sweden.' What a wonderful experience of human compassion. This was 1961, and looking back, hardly speaking English, and with no money, this country was still a lot nicer to live in then. There wasn't much quantity but plenty of quality.

After we left this wonderful lady, we hitched another lift. According to the sign on his van, the driver was a government-employed fellow, and he was heading for Adelaide. What a fantastic run of luck we were having, but of course, when there are so few roads and fewer places they lead to, you can't really go wrong.

Following the Murray River most of the way, it was a very enjoyable trip. We came to the South Australian border, where there was a quarantine checkpoint. 'Anything to declare?' asked the man in charge.

'No,' said the driver, but a long way further down the road when we stopped for a break, he pulled out an esky from underneath some bedding and in it was a pig he had shot.

'The bugger didn't find it,' he said with quite some pride. Putting something over the powers that be is something of a national pastime I was to learn during many years in this country. This sat perfectly with my desire to challenge authority in the name of right and wrong.

The trip along the beautiful Barossa Valley came to an end at Port Adelaide, where we bought the blackest and hardest loaf of rye bread ever made. From there, we got a ride to Port Lincoln, where we decided to spend most of our money on a train ticket to Kalgoorlie in WA. It would've been nearly impossible to hitchhike across the Nullarbor; the road was still dirt most of the way, and there wasn't a heck of a lot of people venturing out there.

We travelled all night and arrived in Kalgoorlie to be met by a clear but cold sky. We took up hitchhiking again: having spent so much money on the train ticket, we had no choice. But it soon became obvious we wouldn't get to Albany in a hurry; there was more wildlife than cars on the road. We kept walking and came to a little mining town by the name of Coolgardie, where the big gold rush in WA began. There was a museum with some fascinating stuff in it. One such thing was an old car that been used as an ambulance in the Middle East during the First World War. It had dual solid rubber tyres widely spaced on a single rim, making the wheel very wide. This clever device stopped the wheels from sinking, making it possible to drive through deep sand. The wide tyres that are used today on off-road vehicles were not invented then. The man who would end up giving me my first mining job, Michael Pietch, tried the same principle using inflatable tyres thirty years later, but it never took off.

We kept walking. There was no traffic of any sort, and when it got close to dark, we decided to make camp. With the experience of nearly freezing to death on the back of that truck fresh in our minds, we dragged together enough firewood to last us a week. The country was turning white with frost, but we'd built a good windbreak and had a roaring fire going, so we were snug.

After a few hours, a truck appeared, but it was going the wrong way. Our camp was fifty metres from the road, so we were surprised when it stopped, and the headlights went out. Shortly after, a figure could be seen walking toward us in the moonlight; it was a man, and he was carrying something. We looked at each other and realised this could mean trouble. We were camped in God knows where, were unable to communicate in the country's language, and frankly, were quite scared. As it turned out, the man was Greek and spoke even less English than us.

The bundle he was carrying, and which we thought might have been a gun, held, among other things, a jar of black olives and a big salami. He offered it to us, and with our rock-hard loaf of rye bread, we had a feast there in the bush. We understood that he'd stopped when he saw the campfire, hoping he could join us and get warmed up. The trucks had no internal heaters in those days and no air conditioning. I'd spend many nights myself when truck driving later in life, shivering cold in the winter and roasting in the summer. After an hour or so, our dinner guest left, and we tried to get some sleep, though this wasn't so easy. There were a lot of strange noises, and this was dingo country. From what I'd read, they could be pretty savage animals.

The next morning as we got back on the road, our luck changed when we got a ride after a couple of kilometres walking.

This ride took us to Perth; we were getting somewhere. We soon learned that city people weren't as friendly as the ones in the country. Nobody offered us a ride, and we walked around twenty kilometres to a suburb named Armadale. From then on, the road is quite steep uphill for about ten kilometres, but we hadn't gone far before an old car stopped. The driver took us to the top of the hill, which turned out to be outside an old pub, and asked us to have a beer with him. We said no: we were broke and had just finished the last bit of the loaf of bread, which had lasted longer than any bread known to mankind. The weather was turning nasty too; it got cold and started to rain. We had no raincoats, and it was still 450 kilometres to Albany and pretty late in the day. The temperature would've been around ten to twelve degrees Celsius.

We were beyond grateful when a utility stopped. The man told us he was going to Albany and we finally arrived there at about 10.00 pm. He knocked on the door of a guesthouse: it was now pouring with rain, and we had to find shelter for the night. After knocking on the door for a while, a very annoyed looking woman opened it and asked our benefactor if he had any idea what time it was and that she was closed. After he'd explained to her that we'd been on the road all day with nowhere to stay, she invited us in. She told us to have a long hot shower, which was heaven. After we'd showered, she turned up with some sandwiches and hot chocolate. 'Who the hell would want to go back to Sweden?' I asked Charlie. 'The people in this country are marvellous!'

CHAPTER 7

# Life on the Land

After breakfast that first morning in Albany, we had a look around town. During our travels, we came to a business area called Pettersson's Plaza. *This chap must have Swedish blood in him somewhere along the line*, I thought. The owner, who the plaza was named after, had a second-hand shop there. This was very lucky; we could buy a tent and pitch it somewhere, saving money on accommodation until the land board had met and we could move on to our land. The fact that we may not get any land didn't occur to us. When Geoff Pettersson, the shop owner, an ex-policeman whose father had emigrated to Australia, heard of our plan to sit out the winter in a tent, he exclaimed: 'You're completely crazy. We get a hell of a lot of rain during the winter, even snow. You're coming home with me when I close the shop, and I'll think of something.'

When we got back to the shop at closing time, he'd loaded his utility with single beds, mattresses, and heavy woollen blankets. 'When I said it's getting cold here in the winter,' he said, 'I wasn't kidding.'

Geoff owned a cottage on the beach at a place called Little Grove. He introduced us to his wife, Nancy, and his daughter, Pauline, and told them we were staying in the garage. After we'd unloaded all the bedding, Nancy came over and told us we were having tea with them over at the house.

We hadn't sat down for a meal since we left Bonegilla, which seemed a lifetime ago. And what a meal! It was the third time I'd eaten ate steak in our new country. Eating meat was a luxury we simply couldn't afford on the family farm. Even though we went hungry at times, the fear poor people like us had for the law was such that most would starve rather than shoot a wild animal out of season, like when one of my uncles shot a woodcock. He was terrified the local police would find out about it, so he crept through the bushes to get it home. It weighed over seven kilograms and fed us for some time. In contrast, I found people in Australia lived on meat!

The following morning at the breakfast table, Geoff told us about his plans for us to work for board and food. Charlie, who had been doing a bit of spray painting in Sweden, could go with him to his shop and paint some fridges and furniture. 'You, Bill, can start cutting down the scrub around the cottage.'

There were seven acres of it. He wanted the boundaries cleared because he had plans to subdivide the lot for housing. 'When you get tired of it, ' he said, 'you can take the boat, set the trap and see if you're any good at fishing.'

Before he left for town, he showed me where the boat was kept. It was a little fibreglass one, small enough to be carried by one man. After working pretty hard for a couple of hours, I went and put the trap in. I figured there should be some fish in it by the end of the day. I toiled hard the rest of the day, and before Geoff and Charlie got back, I went to check the trap. If Geoff

## Chapter 7: Life on the Land

had doubts about my fishing ability, he sure would change his opinion when he saw what I'd caught. There would've been at least a dozen fish in the trap. They were funny looking fish with a spike on their head.

'You've done well, Bill, ' he said. 'We'll have them for tea; they're leatherjackets, a delicious fish!'

Nancy cooked them in milk, and it was indeed a tasty meal, and I felt happy to have been able to contribute something. While we were staying with Geoff and his family, we went with him to the Yacht Club one day. He was a member there, and they'd just built a new clubhouse and were searching for water underground. Charlie and I offered to help drill for water, which was done by hand and on the beach of all places. A heavy steel pipe was used, the bottom end was serrated. It had a giant pipe wrench attached to it with a long extension. This pipe stood up vertically with the serrated end on the ground and turned while water was pumped inside under pressure. This was getting rid of the sand inside the pipe, which made it sink. It was heavy going, but after getting to a depth of about five metres, we found a good supply of drinking water.

After a few days, a big green car pulled up at the cottage, and a lanky man stepped out. 'Anybody home?' he called out.

I was working at the back of the house, and he didn't see me. Not speaking English too well, I stayed hidden: entering into a conversation with a stranger was the last thing I wanted to do. When Geoff got back that afternoon, he asked me if I had seen someone that day. He explained to me that the man was a farmer looking for a farmhand. I felt like a bloody goose then: I wanted a job more than anything, but getting into a car with a stranger was a risk I would not have taken, especially since I would have had no idea what he wanted.

'Don't worry,' Geoff said with that marvellous expression again. 'I'll fix it.'

He rang the farmer and explained the situation. The farmer returned to town the following day—more than 150 kilometres—to pick me up.

The farmer's name was Eric Bungey, and he had a 4,000-acre wheat and sheep farm over a hundred kilometres inland at a place called Gnowangerup. Before Eric arrived, Geoff brought a sailor's kitbag home from the store and proceeded to fill it to the top with clothes and a pair of work boots. There were some very heavy jumpers among them. All I knew about Australian weather was from the promotions that were run in Sweden: sunshine all the time and kilometres of sandy beaches full of bikini-clad babes. I picked up a woolly jumper in front of Geoff, 'I need this?' I asked.

'Believe me,' said Geoff, 'when the wind comes off those mountain peaks, you'll wish you had half a dozen of them.'

He was right, the Stirling Ranges get snow on them in winter, and the wind blows at a steady pace most of the time.

I got the job on the farm thanks to Geoff, who wasn't a successful businessman for nothing. Eric must have thought he'd snared the most qualified farmhand in the western world, and I set out to prove him right. However, whatever I'd been good at in Sweden didn't count for much here. My experience might as well have been gained on the moon.

Not speaking the language was a worry. Eric asked me to wash and polish his car one day, and I wanted to make a good impression and spent a lot of energy on the polishing. The next day when I walked past it, I noticed many scratches on the boot lid; I hadn't seen them when I washed it and was puzzled. Having thought about it, I concluded that I must have done it while I was polishing it. I had been wearing a 'ringers' jacket that had metal studs on it and convinced myself that was the cause of the scratches. I was really worried. I had no idea how I was going to explain this to Eric with my limited English. The car was a big Vauxhall and nearly new, the thought of losing my job on the first day scared the hell out of me, but there was no way I wouldn't tell him. I asked him to come with me to the car and showed him the damages. 'I do that,' I said.

'No, Bill, don't you worry about it,' he said.

I couldn't believe my luck, what a tolerant boss! However, a few days later, Eric called out to me: 'Come here, Bill!'

I ran over to him and on his shiny boot lid was a male turkey kicking the hell out of his car. 'Breeding season,' Eric explained. 'He's fighting his reflection in the lid. He made the scratches. You did too good a job polishing the car.'

That took a lot of weight off my shoulders.

The first day at Bungey's was a revelation. We brought in a mob of sheep, probably 500. I'd never seen a sheep close up before and was getting seasick walking behind them, their bodies moving up and down in slow motion, like waves. They had to be checked for blowfly strikes, which is where the flies lay their eggs. When they hatch, the maggots eat their way into the meat. If not caught in time, it will kill the sheep. This meant a lot of work in the yard, and while sheep might look soft and cuddly, the rams reached a weight of 100 kilograms and would charge you at full speed if you were in their way. Eric warned me the first day I worked in the yard as I stepped in front of them to stop them from getting past. 'They'll snap your legs like they're matchsticks,' he told me.

Seeing the rams fight was awesome. In the breeding season, they would face up to each other, reverse up to ten metres or so, and then accelerate towards each other until their heads met. They would literally bounce off each other, back away, and then repeat the same act. There would be splinters flying from their horns, and after prolonged fighting, they would be worn down to the quick and a lot of blood lost. This in itself was a common area for flystrike. After being checked, the next morning, we started shearing.

Many farmers employed Aboriginal shearers because they were excellent, and plenty were looking for work. The biggest problem was to keep them for any length of time. Their culture never included working for somebody else and has always been nomadic; when the animals they hunted got a bit scarce, they'd move to another area. Sometimes, they'd leave their home district for quite some time, the name for which was 'walkabout'. There was never any prior warning; one morning, they would simply not turn up at the shearing shed. This was a bloody nuisance and caused a lot of friction between farmers and the native shearers. I see another side of it, though. It would be very hard to promote the benefit of employment to Aborigines who'd been surviving for tens of thousands of years without a boss.

When they got stuck in, however, they worked bloody hard. I came across this when truck driving years later. If I were on my way from the depot in Albany late in the afternoon and met either of my two truck driving aboriginal workmates, Lester Coyne and Roy Minister, they'd park up their trucks and come with me to unload mine—it could have been hundreds of kilometres from the depot. We'd then travel back to the depot together. When it was smoko time, we'd share any cakes or sandwiches we had between us. Any offspring of Lester or Roy who might read this can be proud of their fathers; they were the best workmates I ever had.

## Chapter 7: Life on the Land

One Friday, when I was going into town with John, a couple of our shearers asked for a ride. A few kilometres out of town, there was a knock on the truck's rear window, and as John came to a halt, the shearers jumped off and went into the bush. There was nothing but thick foliage around. 'They live here?' I asked.

'No mate, but the tribe in town know exactly when the shearing started and who's working. They'll be waiting for these lads to turn up and help them get rid of their hard-earned money.'

Maybe their walkabout coincided with having a few bob in their pockets. Despite working side by side, I noticed that Aborigines weren't allowed to drink at the same bars as the white man, which upset me seeing that you were allowed to bring your dog with you in some pubs. They were hard workers and great personalities, and it troubled me to see them treated with such disrespect by some parts of the community.

During the shearing on Eric's farm, my job was to pick up the 'belly', where the shearers open the fleece up. Shearing is a very skilled trade; it doesn't take much to cut the skin and is just as easy as cutting yourself shaving. Every shearer had a few needles with lengths of thread hanging next to them to stitch up any sheep who was seriously cut. No doubt some shearers are better than others, and one shearer who spent quite a bit of time stitching up sheep that he'd cut drew this dry remark from Eric: 'I reckon the sheep will have more wool next year if you leave the skin on them.'

When the shearer finished his sheep, Eric or John would rush in and pick up the fleece, and I had to sweep the floor, ready for the next one. I also had to keep the catching pens full. Each shearer had their pen where he caught his sheep, and when the numbers got down to just a few, I had to 'top them up'. It makes it much easier to catch a sheep in a full pen since they've got no room to run away. I also had to collect the fleece and press them into bales once Eric had skirted, that is, removing stained wool or wool that has a lot of grass seed or other impurities in it; classed them, depending on the quality; and put them in several different stacks.

It was a good thing I didn't smoke, as I never had a minute to scratch myself. On the second day, Eric said to me, 'Have a go at throwing a fleece, Bill.'

Well, I was game, and it looked pretty easy when Eric did it. You got hold of the front leg part as you pick it off the floor, squeeze the fleece together while you take it to the sorting table, then you pick the fleece up upside down and throw it upwards and forward like you would a bedsheet while holding on to the legs, and it should land the right way up. However, I put a bit too much effort in, and the fleece overshot the table. It landed on the wall on the other side, and there was I, holding the legs that were once connected to the rest of the fleece. There were lots of cheers from everyone, and this was the topic of conversation in the pub the following Friday night. 'Can this fellow throw a fleece!?' John said when asked how I was getting on. 'The first one he had a go at is still going and could make it to Albany before I get there with the rest of the wool!' Albany was a big wool-selling centre in those days and a very busy port. It has one of the world's best protected natural harbours and is more like a big lagoon.

Everyone gave me a lot of ribbing, which I found quite annoying to start with until I realised that it was a sign of acceptance.

We finished the shearing, and I was put to work clearing a big patch of land, about 1000 acres if my memory serves me right. For this purpose, a small bulldozer—a 'crawler'—was used to pull an implement with long tines ripping the stumps out of the ground. It had a winch fitted to it, and when used simultaneously as pulling, you could get very deep-rooted stumps out of the ground. I put too much strain on it one day and snapped one of the tines. No one there had ever done that before.

Another day I was ploughing with a large, powerful tractor towing a four-metre wide plough. There was an ant nest in front of me, and I lined it up with one of the front wheels. I was travelling at a fair speed and got a shock when the wheel went right over the top of the nest. As it came down on the other side, the tractor got hung up on the power steering and bent the hydraulic ram. This was my first encounter with a termite nest: they are as hard as concrete. I never touched another ant nest. The ram could only travel a short distance one way because of the bend in it, so I drove back to the farm in half circles. One short distance forward, reverse and so on. I had no service truck that day.

It was a very dusty job and the country flat with no landmarks. And because of the dust, it was like driving in the heavy fog, and you were working with headlights only. The trick was to leave the service truck parked with the parking lights on, so when you wanted to return home, you just followed the wheel marks back. They were long days. Most of the time, it was dark before I got back to the homestead. Eric always had a 'King Brown'—a large bottle of beer—on the table to go with my tea, which his wife would have kept hot in the oven for me. However, one night I got home very late and very frozen. Eric reckoned I deserved a whisky. *Bloody good boss*, I thought, but as I was heading out the door, he said, 'Don't forget to milk the cow.'

One wonders why the poor cow didn't dry up between losing one farmhand and employing another. I'd been milking cows for years, and never before had I come across one that didn't dry up if you stopped milking it for some time. I still haven't worked out what breed it was. I knew that Eric had been busy practising his golf in the paddock next to where the cow was kept: maybe it would have been possible to fit in a couple of minutes to milk the cow? A matter of priorities, I suppose.

One evening John knocked on my door. 'Fancy a bit of spotlighting?' he asked.

I had no idea what he was talking about, but anything was better than sitting alone in a freezing room, so I agreed.

'You take the .22,' he said, which was a small calibre rifle. 'I'll do the driving and work the spotlight.'

Off we went. He was driving a fairly new Holden car through the scrub, but that didn't seem to worry him too much. All of a sudden, he waved the light about and said in a low voice, 'Look over there, Bill, a roo. You can't miss from here, get him.'

I'd done a lot of hunting in Sweden and was known as a pretty good shot, but I'd never done any shooting in lights before and missed. 'Never mind,' John said. 'You'll soon get the hang of it.'

I didn't understand what the 'hanging' was all about, but he sounded sympathetic, so I was happy. A little bit further on, we spotted a rabbit on the roadside. 'Get him,' whispered John. 'You can't miss this one. If he gets any closer, I'll have to wind the window up, or we'll have him in the cab with us.'

I missed. At breakfast the next morning, Eric asked how the spotlighting had gone the night before. 'We didn't even get a rabbit,' John said. 'I don't know why Bill left Sweden, but if I was a wild animal, I sure as hell would stay there. Must be the safest place on earth!'

Nobody seemed to care much about my inability to handle a gun, but going to work the next morning, I drove through the same paddock where I'd had a shot at the roo. It looked close in the light but must have been at least 500 metres away. I realised then that I'd been set up for a bit of fun and was starting to warm to the way the locals were having a laugh on my behalf.

When I first started working for the Bungey family, we were carting hay to a big stack for use later in the season when the feed was getting scarce. It was oaten hay in big bales, and it was heavy. When I left Sweden, it had been below -10 °C, yet within a couple of weeks in my new country, I was working in thirty-plus and really suffering.

'This is not hot,' said John. 'What do you do in summer over there? It must hit you hard after a long cold winter.'

'We take salt tablets,' I managed to explain to him.

'Crikey, you eat salt?!' he exclaimed. 'What's next?'

Don't give an Aussie starving for a bit of fun a free kick.

The next morning as we got to the haystack, John threw a twenty-kilogram bag of salt on the ground. It was the very coarse type that you feed livestock. 'There you go, Bill, ' he said. 'That should keep you going till dark.'

Once we'd moved on to our block of land, I was telling my spotlighting experience to an elderly Italian, John Gelfi, who had been allocated land next to ours. He grinned and told me this story:

I had the same thing happening to me many years ago. I'd gone with a couple of workmates on a fishing trip one long weekend, both of them Aussies. One day on the way back to camp after having caught nothing, I heard them talking about me. I was like you, I didn't understand English too good, but I understood enough to realise they were up to some pranks. Up ahead of us were a group of emus. One of the Aussies handed a rifle to me, 'Let's see if you're any good with a rifle,' he said. 'Since we missed out on a fish dinner tonight, we'll get one of those emus. Get the little one at the rear.'

'Why not the big one?' I asked, thinking it would be easier to hit.

'No good, you silly bugger. It's too tough. Get the little one.'

'Yes,' said his mate, 'and shoot it through the head: the skins are worth a bit of money, so we don't want any bullet holes in it.'

The ground was pretty rough, and the old ute was bouncing around a bit. Emus can run as fast as a racehorse and not in a very straight line. Bugger it, I thought, I'll aim for the big one, maybe I'd get lucky. I pulled the trigger, and the little one that must've been running twenty metres to the side fell over. 'Bloody hell!' exclaimed the driver. 'Look at that; this bloke is pretty handy with a rifle.'

He drove up to where the emu laid, and his mate jumped off to get it. He looked up, mouth wide open, 'Jesus,' he said, 'I wouldn't want to mess with this fellow. He shot it straight through the bloody neck.'

Well, I couldn't help taking advantage of the situation and said, 'I'm sorry, but the ute was bouncing around too much.'

'Heck, he really thought we were serious when he was asked to shoot it through the head! He certainly got close. What a crack shot!'

When we got back to camp, I thought my mates were showing a lot more respect than usual. Up to now, I had been the dogsbody, lighting the fire and cooking the meals. Tonight, however, I was told to have a rest, 'You've been doing all the work around the camp up to now. We'll fix dinner tonight,' they said.

We had emu steak that night; it was delicious and much like beef—it's actually called 'poor man's steak'. After dinner, I went to bed early since we were leaving for home first thing in the morning. The Aussies don't like being losers, however, and hadn't finished with me yet. Just before I dropped off to sleep, one of them came over to me carrying the emu skin. 'You shot it. It's only fair you should have it,' he said. 'It makes a good pillow.'

I felt a bit embarrassed then. Those blokes weren't such bad guys after all. He was right about the pillow too, it was very comfortable, but a few hours later, I woke up, itching like hell all over. The emus are riddled with lice, something I hadn't known, and I couldn't see any other way to get rid of them other than having a long bath in the river. After an hour or so, I thought I must have drowned them and snuck back to my bed. One of the guys woke up and asked, 'Where have you been? You're all wet; you haven't been swimming, I hope? The river is full of crocodiles! Didn't we tell you?'

'No,' I said, quite hot under the collar. 'You said nothing about lice either.'

'There are no lice in the river, mate,' he said. Well, I thought to myself, there is plenty of the little bastards there now.

My mates never got to know how I'd managed to shoot that emu straight through the neck, and there was a rumour going around that I was as deadly with a rifle as Buffalo Bill.

John never developed the land he was allocated, and if I remember right, he was a stonemason. On the block he had been assigned, there was a half-built church in natural stone in the middle of the bush. All that stone must have been brought in from far away since there was no suitable material close by. Imagine the hardship. The building site was kilometres from the track, let alone a road. It must have been built in the early 1900s because it had a fair-sized gum tree growing in the middle of it that was twice the height of the building. His dream from memory was to complete the project, but it became impractical because of his age. He also invented a new type of brick, made of concrete but with a surface of marble chips. His block of land was at South Tennessee, between Albany and Denmark in Western Australia, and his new venture would have taken a lot of his time.

Because of the unique method of making bricks he had invented, the chips were sparkling clean even though they were made from wet concrete. The bricks came in a lot of different sizes. This made it very hard for professional bricklayers to work with, so John had to train his own men. They became very popular and used mainly for facades on large buildings, like hotels and banks. I ran into him years later at the Royal Show in Perth, where I was exhibiting livestock. He invited me home to meet his wife and his youngest son. An older son was an airline pilot for Qantas; I'd met him sometime before when he came down with his Dad to inspect the block of land. He had two large industrial sheds where he was making his bricks which he now had a worldwide patent on. They had 'Gelfis Bricks' painted across the roof in very big letters, which you could see as you flew over Perth. This was smart and cheap advertising.

Just after I got the job at Bungey's, the land board was sitting in Albany, which meant we had to appear for an interview. Geoff had us spruce up and told us to let him do the speaking, which was fine with us. He must have done a good job of it since we were allocated 300-plus acres in South Tennessee! Sometime before we were given the land, we were taken around to all the blocks for allocation. The man in charge from the land board was a Mr Brown, a most unlikely public serviceman. He made smoko and boiled the billy over an open fire, which he got started by waving a big hat in front of it for a bit of oxygen. We didn't know how long we'd be away inspecting the land, and it took all day;

we had no food with us. Mr Brown shared his sandwiches with us. He was truly a very nice man.

I got a ride to Albany with John when he took a load of wool to the wool store to have a look at the land we'd been given. The following Sunday, I was lucky enough to get a lift with a relative of my neighbour back to Gnowangerup. He was going back to Perth and took the inland road, which took me relatively close. 'We'll stop at Broomhill for a drink,' he said.

We had a couple, and he took off. 'How far is it to the Gnowangerup turnoff?' I asked the bartender.

'You've gone past it, mate. It's twenty kilometres back the way you came.'

Bill—that was the name of the bloke I'd gotten the ride with—reckoned he knew the countryside. It was the middle of the day, it was hot, and there was no traffic. I walked for hours with no water, which was a big mistake. Even worse, I had no hat.

As I was contemplating my stupidity, a car pulled up, though I was just about past caring by then. 'Where are you going?' the driver asked.

'To Bungey's place,' I told him.

'Hop in. I'm going right past.'

It turned out that he and his family were on their way home from church. Thank God for good Christians! When I walked through the house gate, I met John. 'How did you get back?' he asked.

'I got a ride from Albany.'

'To where?' he asked.

'To the front gate,' I said.

This was another topic of conversation in the pub next Friday. It seemed that the car I got the lift to the front gate with was likely the only one on the road that day.

One night, John knocked on my door, 'Come on, Bill, we got to get some sheep in.'

He had probably told me during the day, but I hadn't understood him. There was a stock market in Gnowangerup the next day, and John wanted to get there early. *It can't be much after midnight*, I thought, and it was pitch black. 'It's too dark,' I said.

'Don't worry. We'll take Rag. He knows what he's doing.'

Rag was a half dingo cross sheepdog. He insisted on walking between myself and his master, something my dogs used to practice on my wife later in life. I knew this because I kept tripping over him. When we got to the paddock, Rag disappeared. 'Stay very still,' John told me. 'Rag will do all the work.'

After a while, I could hear the sheep approaching. Rag knew his job alright, but as he was putting them through the gate, I thought some of them were veering off and moved to the side to cut them off. 'Don't move, Bill,' came the now well-understood order. 'Rag knows what to do.'

Standing there in the pitch-black night, being told not to move, I couldn't help but wonder why the hell he'd dragged me out of bed. Being motionless was something I could have practised quite happily in bed, with more satisfaction for both of us. The answer was getting close. When we got back to the sheep yard, John backed the truck up; it had a big crate on the back and three separate decks. This enabled you to cart a lot of sheep on a relatively small truck. Each floor has spaced, narrow floorboards, which is a very clever idea to make the sheep droppings fall to the floor of the truck where they can be collected.

For some reason, the top floor is loaded first. There were no problems since there is plenty of headroom to move around while pushing the sheep into small pens. This is to stop the sheep from 'bunching up', a tendency they have got. They tend to climb on top of each other, resulting in the sheep at the bottom being suffocated. The top deck was full, and John told me to crawl around on all fours and fill the pens on the second floor. Of course, Rag could have done this, but he couldn't slide the bolt that keeps the gates closed. I was surprised to know sheep are very nervous when penned up, so all the feed and water they'd consumed during the day was now being purged. The spacing between the floorboards was exactly right; there were no blockages anywhere, so I was covered in green droppings and warm showers. The bottom deck was an experience no human being should have to go through.

I had purchased a very smart looking straw hat called a Panama hat in a port somewhere along the voyage, and it was the envy of everyone who saw it, judging by the smart remarks it caused. Well, it was anything but smart now, hanging down covering half my face like every Aussie farmers' hat. Up to that time, I hadn't thought much about the origin of this icon. It would seem that it is a pretty accurate barometer for estimating a farmer's wealth: the sloppier and smellier the hat, the more sheep he owns. Imagine the confusion for the poor 'blowies' who were used to attacking the backsides of sheep, an area they'd locate by the smell. To make it easier to tell the difference, some sheep farmers tie lengths of strings with bits of cork on the ends to their hat brims to denote their status. Brilliant idea: when you shake your head, it keeps the flies away, and you don't have to wash your hat! Judging by some of them, that must have been a mortal sin. Now that we had loaded the sheep, it was time for breakfast—the rest of the day passed in a haze.

The next morning there was a knock on the door. It was early, and we were having breakfast. *Who can this be?* Everyone was puzzled.

'Come in,' Eric said.

In came a bedraggled looking man. It was the neighbour who had been shearing his sheep at our place and who had given me a lift the day I came back from Albany. He was usually a very natty dresser in a three-piece suit and a hat with a feather in it. Today, however, he had a strange smell about him: he didn't smell like a sheep farmer at all.

'Please,' he asked Eric's wife, 'can I have a cuppa tea and a shower? My missus'll kill me if I come home looking like this.'

'Where did you come from?' asked Eric. 'You're a long way from home.'

As it turned out, Alec, I think his name was, had been at the sheep market the day before, and those guys make a day of it when they get a chance. He'd spent the whole day at the pub, and when he came back from a 'pitstop' (the loo) he realised the people he was going home with had left. They probably thought he got a ride with someone else.

There he stood, shivering in his three-piece suit. How the hell was he going to get back home? His thinking capacity diminished from a full day on the drink; he was getting worried until he spotted John's truck. There was no sign of John, though, and he sauntered over to the truck. There was a big heap of straw on the floor in the back of the truck. Remember, the wind inland in WA goes right through you, so Alec, feeling the cold badly, crept into the straw to keep warm until John turned up. Having been on ale medication all day, he was drowsy and fell asleep. When he woke up, he realised he must've spent the night in the back of the truck and was now at Eric's place.

That's not the full story, however. John had bought several sows at the market the day before, which is why he had all the straw in the back. Alec, waking up from what he thought was his wife making amorous advances and still being a pretty fit man, started to respond. He got a huge shock when he turned over and looked into a face which was nothing like the one in his wedding photos: it was a sow nudging him. This episode remains one of my favourite memories.

The job at the Bungey's was coming to an end. We were impatient to get a start clearing the land we'd been allocated, and one morning Charlie turned up in a little utility to pick me up.

'Take one of the pups with you,' said Eric. 'You can't farm without a dog.'

Not only did I score a nice looking pup, but I also got a cheque from Eric for the entire time I'd worked. He had said to me after the first couple of Friday nights at the pub with the boys, 'I'll put all your wages in the bank for you, or you'll never get that land of yours cleared.'

He recognised that I had problems putting the brakes on once I'd started drinking. That was one of the prime reasons I left Sweden. What a thoughtful man, and how lucky I was to have been working for him.

CHAPTER 8

# The Australian Dream

Well, if I'd thought that my quarters at Bungey's were primitive, I was in for a surprise. When Charlie and I got to our block of land, it had a little masonite hut on it next to the road. Charlie might've been a good sailor, but he was a lousy builder, though no worse than me. There were several sawmills in the area, and you could get big loads of face cuts, which is the part of the log the miller starts on before he gets into the good timber. Those boards are too small to run through the mill again to put on a straight edge, but they were very useful for a new settler and cheap. When we started buying a few supplies in Albany, the nearest town, we got to know the shop manager. He was a Dutchman by the name of John Deik. He was very helpful and introduced us to the owner of the business, Hector Bell. He was a mason and a very compassionate man. When the sheds at his business were upgraded, he told us we could have all the old roofing iron and any old bolts and nails that could be re-used. He even lent us his big truck to practice on for our Australian drivers' licence. Having met a man like that made me very impressed with the Masonic movement.

It was summer now, and the hut was like an oven. There was also a problem with flies; Western Australia has the friendliest flies in the whole world! They get in your eyes, up your nostrils, in your mouth, and anywhere there was moisture. Wearing shorts was very brave! It was nearly impossible to do a job where you needed both hands: the moment you stopped shooing them away with one hand, your eyes and mouth would be full of them. Some people would hang strings with corks attached to the end of them from their hat brim, working a bit like a horse's mane and shooing the flies off when you shake your head.

Charlie and I went to a shearing school in Fremantle, a city in WA, when we first came to our block of land. The place we stayed at was run by a big, tough-looking Yugoslav who had a scar covering his face from top to bottom. Five other people were staying there. One evening, when I dressed to go out into town, I couldn't find a rather large note of money, ten pounds from memory. I told our landlord, who got very upset. His niece was working as a cleaning lady, and he thought we suspected her of stealing the money. Since we didn't speak the language and were unable to discuss the matter in a civilised way, he called the police. On arrival, the policeman asked if the landlord suspected anybody staying at his place. The big Yugoslav pulled a big knife out of his boot, made a slashing gesture across his throat and said, 'If I suspect, I fix.'

The policeman looked horrified at him. 'For Christ's sake, don't do that,' he said. 'Ring us!'

The last night I stayed in that place, I found the missing note in a pair of boots; it must have fallen in when I was moving the clothes about. When I told the big man, he hugged me. 'I knew my niece is not a thief,' he said.

## Chapter 8: The Australian Dream

Later that evening, he came into our room with a whole cooked chicken and a couple of bottles of beer. 'I'm so happy you found money,' he said, 'and telling me. I knew my niece was innocent.'

Charlie had a job in town working for a car spray painter, and I had to find work pretty quick since we needed the money. As luck would have it, there was a big abattoir in Albany called Thomas Borthwick and Son, and it was the busy season. I got a job straight away and was earning good money. Many women were working there: big Russians and others from the Eastern Bloc, most of them with only a little English. One of my workmates commented that I should take one or two back to the block of land I was clearing. 'You wouldn't need a tractor,' he joked.

One day the foreman, Jack McQueen, came over and told me we would be working back a couple of hours every day for a week or two to catch up on work. I managed to tell him that I had no way of getting home as Charlie knocked off at five, but I promised him I would be right from the next day on.

'Right,' he said, 'I can't afford to be one man down.'

When we got home that evening, we built what was, in essence, a big coffin, but instead of a lid, it had a sliding door on the side. We brought it to Charlie's place of work and were allowed to park it in the backyard. There was a water pipe handy too, so I'd wash under it when I finished work and then crawl into my coffin and sleep until morning. It wasn't very flash, but I hung on to my job. Jack McQueen, having observed how I solved the travelling dilemma, was impressed. The slaughtering season finished after a few months, but he drove out to our block of land at the start of the next season to tell me the job was mine if I wanted it. That was forty kilometres on rough roads; imagine something like that happening today.

While we were busy trying to cram enough hours into a day to get everything done, we had a letter from Arvid Berggren, an old pensioner who had come out on the same ship as us. He had travelled to Australia to spend his last days with his son and his wife. But things didn't work out, and he asked if we would consider allowing him to join us on our block of land. He considered himself pretty handy on a farm and thought that he could be of some use. He was pretty open-minded about most things, and we had enjoyed his company very much on our trip over. We thought it was worth a try and asked him to join us, which turned out to be one of our smartest decisions.

There was nothing this old, one-time small farmer from the north of Sweden couldn't do. He built us a nice little cottage and grew enough vegetables to keep us fully supplied and some for our neighbours. Since we were forty kilometres out of town, he found himself very isolated. 'Buy me a car, and then I can go to the local shop when I want something,' he said.

Nobody worried about a driver's licence in the country in those days. We found him an old car which he then proceeded to repair. For a man who had only had a pushbike for transport his whole life, he was very good at it and soon got hold of an old car for spare parts.

One day went over to another farm that we had taken over from a local man who could not fulfil the Agricultural Department's requirements under which he acquired the land. He followed us over in the car that he had reconditioned. The road was very winding and narrow, and when we came to one very sharp bend, he was unable to slow down: he had put the brakes together wrong. The result was Arvid going through the fence and rolling the car. We had kept an eye on him on the way since we thought that he was going too fast, and as we got to the

## Chapter 8: The Australian Dream

upside-down car, we were worried about the state he would be in. He crawled out with a big grin on his face. 'Well,' he said, 'even an old pensioner can roll a car.'

He was in his seventies but very fit. If any of Arvid's offspring read this, we have got a lot to thank him for. He was a very religious man and would've suffered in our company, but he was an amazing man who taught me many things.

One night, I woke up hearing Charlie yelling something. He came running in through the door with our dog howling behind him. It was a stray he'd brought home from Albany. 'Look out,' he yelled. 'The dog's gone mad!'

He sounded terrified, so I jumped on top of my bed with my torch and the rifle that I'd grabbed from under the bed, where I always kept it. As the dog came through the door, he landed on the veranda. As it came into our room, I had the torch lit. In the light, her eyes were bright red, and she was slobbering from the mouth. I was convinced she had rabies and shot her on the spot. John would've been proud of my marksmanship that night.

Arvid had woken up and come into our room. When he saw the dog in a pool of blood, he gave us a condemning look. 'You are barbarians,' he said.

I could not convince him that I'd feared for our lives. I found out afterwards that Australia doesn't have rabies, and many years later found out why the dog had behaved in such a threatening manner. We'd been out shooting bronze wing pigeons for Christmas dinner and had fed the bones to the dog. The pigeons had been feeding on a berry that contained a poison, similar to the one used for baiting rabbits (1080). It attacks the nervous system, which sends the animals crazy, and they die from heart failure. The birds were immune to this poison and stored it in their bone marrow. How close I was to ending my days at that dinner; I usually like to chew the chicken bones, but the pigeon's bones were a lot harder and too small to bother with.

One day a young Swedish lad turned up. We had a few visits like that over the years from sailors who'd jumped ship. He asked if he could stay for a while. He came from the same area as Arvid, so we thought he would be good company for him. After a week or two of doing very little around the place, we told the young bloke that our neighbour needed workers to pick his potato crop. It was hard work but very well paid. Arvid offered to have a go as well, 'I could do with a bit of money,' he said.

The next morning, the young fellow wasn't very keen to get started, 'My back is killing me,' he moaned. Arvid, who had picked more bags of potatoes than the young lad the day before, turned on him. 'You haven't got a back!' he roared. 'Just a couple of miserly sinews that your arse is tied to!'

We told Lars that if he wouldn't pick potatoes, there was plenty of other work, and if he wanted just to lay back and watch the world go by, book into a holiday resort. He left the following day.

Not far from our block was a smallholding belonging to Bert Martin and his wife, Ailsa. They had four children, three girls and a boy. Bert was a very skilled repairman and could fix just about anything. I'm sorry we didn't show more appreciation for his skill and willingness to help anytime, regardless of how busy he was. He made a living from milking cows, growing potatoes, and sometimes working away driving bulldozers. During such times, his wife would run the farm. We were fortunate to have run into the Martins early in the piece since we got a lot of assistance from them in many ways. Bert would help us out if we broke some implement, and Ailsa made a pretty mean ice cream. We'd supply the eggs, and I think she made it with Carnation milk. If Bert

## Chapter 8: The Australian Dream

had been lucky when fishing, he'd give us a salmon, as would most of the neighbours. I met Barbara in 1962 when calling in on her father, Bert, to get a machine repaired.

The eldest girl in the family, Barbara, was pretty good on the piano accordion. I played the trumpet and the saxophone, and a young boy on a farm some distance away also played the accordion, if I remember right. We would often get together to practice and play together, and after some time, Barbara and I found we also had other interests. One thing led to another, and in what seemed a very short time, we were married. We were very much in love, we thought, but looking back, I realise that it was probably more to do with raging hormones.

It could have worked out okay, but we were both away with the fairies, daydreaming about making things live up to our expectations. The cold turkey treatment of going from party animal to no partying at all proved too much for me to cope with. It was a hell of a cultural shock. My personality changed from being an outgoing young man who thought life was just one big opportunity to a self-centred individual who had one thing on his mind: get my own farm. If it hadn't taken me fifty years to realise my problems, a lot of heartaches might have been avoided. I should have taken more notice of the retired schoolteacher who came out on the same boat. She told us there was no nightlife in Australia after 6.00 pm and that the beaches had 'beach masters' employed to make sure that men and women didn't swim together. I thought she was bullshitting, but we spent a couple of nights in Port Adelaide when we first arrived at an Australian port, and the statement about the 6.00 pm curfew was spot on. The beach masters part I never figured out since we never had any time during the day to spend on the beach. Looking at beaches today, I guess things have changed somewhat.

I had made a great friend in Michael, a young boy suffering the after-effects of polio. He had improved to such an extent that he got himself a car, a job and a lovely girlfriend. Tragically, as he was driving down York Street in Albany one day, he slumped over dead at the steering wheel. That was a shock to all of us. When we were practising our music, we alternated between Barbara's home and Michael's. It was an opportunity for their parents to get together as well, but that came pretty much to a stop after Michael's death.

We did have another pastime, table tennis, and we played in the local hall, where quite a few people used to turn up. I really enjoyed my farming days in South Tennessee, and it was a pity I couldn't express my appreciation at the time. Not being fully conversant with the language, it was hard to participate in the local life. Having been burned a couple of times because of our poor understanding of the language, we kept our distance.

We'd hired a bulldozer operator to clear our block of land when we first got there, and we were informed he charged an hourly rate. 'I'll clear a lot in an hour,' the operator said.

But when we came home from work to our plot, there was hardly anything done. 'How much you clear?' I asked.

He gave me a figure, and I went and stepped it out.

'Bullshit.' That was one word I spoke fluently. 'You trick us.'

'That's the trouble with you foreigners; you don't understand the way we measure things in this country,' he said.

I had no argument with him there. 'You finish,' I said. 'No more.'

'Wait a minute my friend, we got a verbal contract to clear your land at so much an hour, I'll be back tomorrow,' he said.

'You come back, clear everything, we not pay.'

## Chapter 8: The Australian Dream

He didn't come back. We told our mentor, Geoff Pettersson, about our run-in with this guy. 'Don't worry, I'll find someone else,' he said.

We met with a very nice man named Geoff Howie, and he offered to clear the land for an amount per acre. This was fantastic. We now knew that regardless of the time it took him to clear an acre, the cost would be the same. He got very upset when we asked for a signed written agreement. 'I have never done a job where I have been asked to sign a contract,' he said. 'What's wrong with a man's handshake?'

Again, Geoff saved our skin, explaining to him how we'd been conned before, '... but of course, it's in your interest as well, you don't know anything about these fellows.'

He brought out two dozers which pulled a heavy chain between them, knocking over the stunted trees and scrub as if they were cutting grass.

One family, Tim and Meg Wolfe, are worth a special mention. They owned land next to our block, where they grew potatoes and ran sheep. Tim pulled up at our hut one day just after we'd bought the land. He told us that we got a raw deal, 'This land is very acidic,' he told us, 'and if you try to plough it and bring up the acidic ground, nothing will grow for a long time.'

I asked why the farmers weren't putting lime on the ground. 'What difference does that make?' he asked.

'I will show you,' I said. 'I'll dig in lime on a small patch and plant some clover. It will grow, I guarantee it.'

I dug the patch over, put a good dressing of hydrated lime down, and the result was amazing. The clover grew ankle-deep in no time, and when Tim came past some months later, he was most impressed. 'If lime makes that much difference, you can have as much as you need to establish your pasture from my place,' he said. 'I've got massive sandhills on my property that contains over eighty per cent calcium. I'm sitting on a gold mine once the farming community wakes up to the benefit of lime!'

He kept his word; we carted 130 tonnes onto our virgin land and grew pasture instantly.

I should probably take the opportunity to say a few words about Charlie here. Spreading the lime sand was done by a spreader made by a Danish blacksmith to my specification from the rear axle of a utility, which is a small truck, usually about one ton. The differential was made to point upwards with a large circular plate bolted to it. This was turned by the forward movement of the machine, as the wheels were turning the 'diff'. The machine had a large hopper to hold the lime sand and a grill on top to separate the hard calcified lumps that would have wrecked the machine. This resulted in us having to load by hand, a bloody hard job with all those lumps.

Charlie and I were evenly matched and always competing; we loaded and spread thirty tons of lime one weekend. No one but Charlie would've been able to keep up with me. He was a big unit of a man, had been a sailor for many years and was quite a bit older than me. He would go down to the harbour when there was a Swedish ship in port and often came back with bits and pieces that were surplus to their requirements. Heavy wire ropes were very handy on the farm. We'd tie a heavy log behind the tractor and drag it along. This would break the vegetation, and when summer and the hot weather came along, it would die off, and we would then burn it.

Going back to our meeting with Tim and his offer of free lime, I had a win in more ways than one. Since the land needed so much more work put into it, I thought we could get something knocked off the price. I sat down and wrote a letter to the Land

Department and told them about our problems. They earned my respect: not only did they manage to decipher my letter, but they also informed me that after due consideration, it was decided to cut the purchase price by fifty per cent. In those days, a stamp cost five pence, and it would no doubt be the best investment I'd ever made.

I met Tim's son many years later, and he told me that he was busy supplying lime all over the place. 'A bloody good money earner and you fellows started it! Look at the paddocks, Bill,' he said.

Where it used to be poor pasture and bracken fern, it was now a lush pasture. It made me feel pretty good. Remember, Australia fifty years ago was pretty much in the Stone Age when it came to the scientific side of farming. Tim's son, also named Bill, was about the same age as me but died quite young, and his son Darren is now running the farm. I still keep in touch with the family, and Darren married my niece, Samantha.

When the meat work closed until the next season, I was looking for a job. As luck would have it, a neighbour of ours, Arthur Jarvis, did some contract fencing for the farmers in the district. Arthur was also in the same situation as us and needed the income to develop a block of land, so he came over to our hut and asked if I could help him out. He'd been given a big fencing job on a cattle stud, Springfield Grazing Company, but the owner, Percy Nicholson, wanted him to work with the livestock as well. This man was scared of cattle, especially since he was supposed to tame some pretty big bulls good enough to take them to sales and shows. 'I'm no good with animals,' he said, 'but if you take the job with the livestock, I'll do the fencing.'

He gave me directions to the farm, which was a kilometre cross country from the road Charlie travelled to work on every morning. This would work out alright: he could drop me off in the morning at the roadside, and I'd walk across the country to the farm, and then he'd pick me up again at night. We only had that one little utility between us.

When I explained to the stud owner at the Springfield Grazing Company that I wanted the job with his bulls, he told me it was already taken 'by a bloke from out your way'. He was going to confirm it that day.

'He only want the fencing job,' I explained. 'He is scared of the bulls.'

'No,' Percy Nicholson, the farmer, said. 'The two jobs go together; since he didn't bother telling me you can have the job, are you sure you can handle it?'

It was one thing I was sure of: handling livestock was something I'd done all my life. He was very impressed when I walked into a pen with a ton worth of bull in it and started brushing it down. 'You'll do,' he said. 'We start at seven in the morning.'

So I started my job as a stud groom. This was a job I was very qualified for and was the first opportunity I'd had to practice many of the things I'd learned at the agriculture college; the right type of feed for different aged cattle is one of many. Percy had been without someone to tend to the animals for a while, and some of the bulls were huge. Some were partly tamed, and others were not.

Around that time, we had bought an old Fordson Major tractor that ran on kerosene, and a new offset plough. The ground was so acidic that none of the local farmers ploughed the land for fear of bringing up too much acidic soil: an offset disc plough was the answer. The front set would turn the soil one way. The rear set would turn it back. This meant that all the roots of the plants we were trying to get rid of were cut off, and the topsoil remained on top. When the neighbours saw how well this worked, we got plenty of contract ploughing, which was welcomed since we needed plenty of money to develop our block of land. Since we both had permanent jobs, there was no solution other than to spend alternative nights on the tractor, ploughing. Becoming a big-time farmer was turning into an obsession.

The first morning at work, Percy asked me to take a big roan bull to water: we had to lead them there. Having spent the night on the tractor, I was probably not as alert as usual, especially around some pretty big bulls I knew very little about. As soon as I got to the door with the beast, he went right over the top of me, and we landed in the sludge outside. As I looked back to see what Percy thought about this less than impressive start by his new man, all I could see was a big grin and realised in a flash that I'd been set up.

I was very fit, and a bit peed off, and decided I'd stay with the bull until one of us were broken. After being dragged through the lush green grass and even greener manure, the bull came to a stop. After some quiet talking to him, we started for home. He tried a couple more times to get away, but his heart wasn't in it. As I led him into the yard, Peter, Percy's son, yelled out, 'Well done, Bill! It's the first time anyone led that bull back.'

That acknowledgement just about made up for the state I was in; green all over and smelly. I had a battle getting a ride back home that night!

I got my revenge at the bull sale the following year. We'd just arrived at Claremont showground and were unloading the bulls. Percy, who had arrived there the day before and had been having a few drinks with his mates, offered to help me. For some reason, he went right over to the bull that had been taking me for a ride, and I pointed out to him that he'd better take another one. 'Hell,'

Percy looked around to his mates, 'he's giving me orders now. If a man can't manage his own animals, he's in the wrong game!'

Percy was an older man and should have known better, but drinking with his mates all day had made him overly optimistic. Down the ramp he went, and as soon as they reached the ground, the bull took off and didn't stop until he found some other animals a few sheds away. I kept a straight face, I needed a job, and I liked this one. My job here was going nicely, and I stayed for quite a while. After a time, however, Percy and I had different views on best preparing his cattle for show, and I left.

He'd given me bonuses over the couple of years I worked for him. The first year the bonus was a shearing plant that came in very handy when we bought our first sheep. The second year, at about the same time we parted company, he gave me a purebred Poll Shorthorn bull, and since we'd started to get some cattle, it was a most welcome bonus. He also did not hesitate to give me a good reference. It was Christmas, a perfect time to get rid of someone, and I was happy to try something else.

There was a big trucking company starting up in Albany called Brambles. I made some enquiries and got started as a crane driver. I'd married Barbara and lived on the land that the government had allocated Charlie and me. Charlie and I had split the land that we occupied in half. We had some animals, but when I got this job, Barbara was staying home and tending to them. She was very qualified in all sorts of farming, having managed a dairy farm on her own among various other jobs at just over sixteen years of age. It would be a fair hike into town to the Brambles depot, and it was a drag, alright, having to travel forty kilometres before and after work.

CHAPTER 9

# Living on the Road

When I started driving long distance for Brambles in 1969, there wasn't much time for sleep. It was very good money, but the trade-off was that I had no family life. The first year I clocked up more than 150,000 kilometres and quite often slept under the truck on the side of the road in the summer. In those days, everything that was needed out east in the way of building materials, fuel, and fertilizers, had to come from Albany. There weren't even bunkering facilities in Esperance and very few small businesses.

We used to cart all types of small goods on top of our loads of drum fuel—small cabinets, even cakes and specially ordered goods. There would've been millions of kilometres covered during a five to ten year period. Brambles had a fleet of three semitrailers and four to five flat tops, and a couple of cranes at the depot in Albany.

Although it pains me to say it, discrimination was never far from the surface. Lester Coyne and Roy Miniter, two of my favourite colleagues, were targeted because of their colour. To a lesser extent, I was too because of my limited English.

Being Swedish, I was called Turnip. I could never understand this hang-up about colour. We're all born colourblind, and yet somehow, many adults of those times were quick to judge and discriminate against anyone who was not like them.

Lester has achieved an enormous amount in the community and has a lot of knowledge about the subject that is closest to the First Nations peoples' heart - the preservation of their land. He shared his detailed memories of our time with Brambles and the type of work we were contracted to do, which I wanted to share:

When I first joined Brambles, I came from driving trucks for Mayne Nickless. The Brambles manager was Andre Geddes. He was a good free-flowing young manager. Our fleet of trucks consisted of mainly Thames Trader prime movers and single axle trailers with a top speed of 70km/h with windows that didn't wind up or down. We had one inter semi and a V8 Thermodyne Mack prime mover for the fuel run.

A trip to Esperance in a Thames Trader with a full load of shearing shed timber for a farmer or 44-gallon drums of fuel for Ravy or Hopetoun Munglinup was long and tedious. The Philips River 20kms west of Ravensthorpe was all gravel, so our old trucks were down to low gear when going down the steep road into the Philips River, which flooded during winter. The ride out of the river bed and up the other side was slow and would easily take twenty minutes off the trip, and if you lost your load due to rocks sticking out of the road surface or load shift, there was an even greater delay. But there was some help on hand as in the bushes on the side of the Philips was an old unused Fordson tractor with a front end loader bucket on, so we could put the load back on. That area is now a two-lane sealed highway.

When I started, Brambles were contracted to shift hundreds of tonnes of bagged cement from the rail yards to behind the

## Chapter 9: Living on the Road

cattle sale yards on lower Denmark Road for Robins Concrete, a concrete batching mixing company. Robins were building all of the new wool stores to accommodate Albany's burgeoning business, and with no bulk cement, all their mixing was done using thousands of bags of cement. These had to be loaded out of rail trucks onto our trucks, then off our trucks into Robins Concrete storage.

We also carried thousands of earthenware pipes to Sandover's, a hardware store next to the Albany Courthouse, in addition to 7000 tonnes of urea from the port to Albany highway, and bagged flour for Day Bros bakers. All required heavy, repetitive lifting.

All bobtail and semi drivers, except for fuel tanker driver Keith Knoakes and Hiab driver Fred Byatt, were expected to load and unload all bagged goods. Drivers going to Esperance were usually expected to bring bales of wool back from Esperance, and each bale was then compressed and bound by steel wire into smaller tighter bales for overseas markets. In effect, we bought the wool over, then, after compressing, took each bale to the wharf for shipment overseas.

If returning from Esperance, Hopetoun or Ravensthorpe, a return trip usually consisted of empty 44-gallon drums from various fuel outlets in the region. My time with Brambles was hard but interesting work, and I made and kept good friends as a result.

Reading Lester's recollection brought back a memory of Andre coming down to the railway station one hot, sunny day. We had hundreds of tonnes of cement in 25-kilo bags that had to be handled twice, and it was a horrible job that everyone hated. Seeing how slow we were progressing that day as we sweltered in the heat, Andre says, 'Well boys, we are getting nowhere at a hell of a pace.'

Brambles carted most of the fuel and building material needed for the extensive development around Esperance and Albany. I had a fuel run that most of the time entailed a 1000-plus kilometre round trip. There were no logbooks in those days!

Many roads were unsealed, or in terrible condition and on one occasion, I hit a very deep pothole, and one of the fuel drums fell off the back. The hole the fuel drum made in the road was deep enough to reverse into! I pulled up a timber road post to roll the fuel drum back on the truck again. The next truckie that came along could see where it had fallen off. A drum of fuel weighs over 200 kilos, and he was quite sceptical when I told him I'd lifted it back onto the truck again in a fit of rage.

During my time with Brambles, I met the man in charge of bombing the Nazi headquarters in Copenhagen towards the end of the war. He was Air Chief Marshall Sir Basil Embry, and there was a television documentary made about him and the raid. The mission was to wipe out the Nazi headquarters, where secret files were known to be kept and included information about the allies fighting capacity and plans. It was very dangerous, and the big bombers flew below chimney levels at times to evade radar. The squad knew before they set out on the mission that some prisoners would be held at the location, but the order was to erase the building. The prisoners would've been killed by the Germans anyway after being severely tortured to reveal the names of people the Germans wanted. Sir Basil was given land under the same conditions as me and spent the first couple of years camped under a big gum tree with a large tarpaulin draped over one branch.

Delivering some building materials to his block of land east of Albany, I was invited to take tea with him and his wife. To meet a man like Sir Basil Embry and be told that he was developing virgin land like me, getting no favours, despite what he'd done for

## Chapter 9: Living on the Road

his country, was very sobering. He told me that he was struggling and asked if the company I worked for needed more drivers; he had a son who needed a job—what a remarkable man.

Brambles even had the contract to spread the fertilizer needed for all the land the Americans were developing. Among the famous Americans developing land were dancer Ginger Rogers, television personality Alf Linkletter, and American bank chairman Chase Bunker. There was also an enormous property being developed east of Esperance, the Australian equivalent of King Ranch in Texas, USA. I was personally involved with delivering fuel and other commodities to those famous people and carting wool back to the Albany wool store to be sold. A lot of that wool had to be loaded off the ground since a number of properties did not have a shearing shed on them. Most of the wool bales would be over two hundred kilos in weight, and there were thousands of them.

When you've loaded a full load from the ground and stacked the bales three high, you know you've been working. It wasn't just the hard work, though. If there was a problem, there were no mobile phones. When I first started working, there were also no two-way radios. Once we'd had a lot of rain, all the creeks, of which there were plenty, were flooded, and we had a deadline to get the wool to the Albany wool sale. A lot of that wool had to be picked up more than 500 kilometres away from Albany. There were hardly any man-made crossings, so you had to keep on top of the big flat stones in the creek beds. I got over the creek, but the farm manager had been making a new road on the other side, and it hadn't had time to compact. I bogged the truck. It was still pouring with rain, and I was thirty kilometres from anywhere. I hadn't had anything to eat for most of the day since I would be back out before dark. There was nothing to do but curl up in the cab and wait for the morning, hoping the rain would stop by then and I could get out. It was bitterly cold, and I couldn't light a fire since everything was soggy and wet. When morning came, it had stopped raining. I managed to get out of the bog and drove in the scrub on the side easily since it was flat country, but after less than a hundred metres, I sank again, this time for good. I remembered having seen a homestead on the way in from the main road and started walking back.

After a couple of hours, I could see a building in the distance. Walking up on the big veranda, I hoped someone was home. I was starving, thirsty, and of course, needed someone with a big tractor to get me out of the bog. A large man came to the door, 'What do you want?' he asked.

I explained to him that I was picking up wool from one of the big sheds, had become bogged, and could he give me a pull to get out. In a very educated, upper-class voice, this Englishman told me that the tractors on the place were used only for farming purposes. After another hour or so, I came to a block of land a new settler like myself was busy clearing. When he heard of my problems, he unhooked the implement he was using, gave me a drink out of his canvas bag, and off we went. I gave him my invoice book and told him to write out one to Brambles for the two hours it took to get me out of the bog. I got in trouble over that later; the manager reckoned he should have done it free of charge. Some people are hard to understand. I could have asked this guy to take me to the roadhouse some distance away and call for one of the cranes to come out from the nearest depot, a round trip of 140 kilometres and an hourly rate of $70.00. Brambles were one of the biggest trucking companies in the country. I didn't pick up any wool from that shed because I couldn't get to it.

## Chapter 9: Living on the Road

Barbara had now started work at the Albany wool store, bringing in some welcome money. We'd see each other when I was bringing a load of wool in from out east, where the Americans had developed millions of acres of virgin land under the same conditions as ours. Not all of the developing schemes that the government had instigated were of benefit to the settlers. Some of the land was completely unsuitable for farming, especially out east, where enormous tracts of land had been allocated for wheat farming. The land was very poor, and there was some sort of disease in the crops.

I carted timber for buildings to one of those poor guys. He'd been allocated thousands of acres of land for grain production and was an immigrant from Czechoslovakia, as it was in those days. To develop all this land, he'd sold his trucking business at Wongan Hill in Victoria, more than a dozen trucks, and spent most of the money planting a wheat crop, having a very good season. However, when it came to harvest the crop, the wheat board in WA had an oversupply of wheat from farmers: they solved the problem by introducing a quota system, where the growers were given a certain amount to deliver. This seems fair enough until you realise the established growers had no restrictions put on them at all. The poor bastards that had put their life's work into developing all that land didn't get enough quotas to pay for the planting of the crops. That particular farmer I mentioned before had an enormous crop but no buyers, and the grain was falling on the ground as the crop ripened. He was in such a bad way he couldn't even get finance to put livestock on it. It proves again that if you have the right contacts, your abilities are not that important. The poor new starters were cut loose to fend for themselves while the wealthy farmers got looked after.

After a couple of years of driving long distance, I was offered an easier job in town. It did not work out, however, mainly because the whole fleet was equipped with two-way radios, and I, used to being on the open road and planning a lot of my trips on my own, couldn't stand the office staff frequently checking up on me because they had nothing else to do. One weekend I had off, I drove to a stud farm whose owner, Greg, had asked me several times to come and take care of his Poll Shorthorn beef cattle stud. I was fed up with having to listen to the crap on the two-way radio, and we came to an agreement where he would provide a cottage, milk, meat, and thirty dollars per week. I was also to get five per cent of the bull sales. This breeder had bought most of his foundation stock from Percy Nicholson, so I knew that he had top quality cattle. Money was no object with this breeder; he wanted results and told me that I had free hands to do whatever was required to raise animals that would win shows. I went to work selecting the most suitable animals and started feeding them as much that they could eat. We had one young bull that put on six kilograms per day for three months running, that was a couple of kilos more than any other breed being tested for weight gain on properties in the wheat belt.

During my time with Springfield Grazing company we supplied Poll Shorthorn heifers to mate with the Santa bulls at King Ranch, after a few crosses, the offspring were pure Santa Gertrudis. After just a few crosses, the offspring was registered as pure Santa Gertrudis. King Ranch is world-famous for its quarter horses and Santa Gertrudis cattle studs, the biggest in the world. They developed in the order of one and a half million acres in the first few years.

At the Claremont showground the following year, we had the highest scoring exhibit ever shown at that ground. Percy

## Chapter 9: Living on the Road

Nicholson himself came up to me and told me I had done a fantastic job. I felt very proud, but also sad I hadn't been able to have the same success with his animals. We both knew why. Percy was a wealthy man but would not part with the money required to pay for the feed I needed for the animals to compete successfully. The reason for this could have been the hardship he'd endured during his life. He was gassed during World War I and had enlisted at sixteen years of age. He fossicked for gold after his return and developed a sheep stud on a big property outside Williams in WA. It was the first Romney Marsh stud in the state. He also started the first Poll Shorthorn beef cattle stud at Springfield Grazing Company, near Albany. He was cautious with money, to his downfall, as it turned out.

The following year, Greg Dunkle averaged one thousand dollars more per head at the Claremont bull sale than he got the year before when he'd been managing his herd. We sold sixteen bulls, so I was looking forward to a nice commission. However, I saw another side to Greg, who backpedalled on our deal. 'When I said that you would get five per cent on the bull sales,' he said, 'I never thought we would make that much money. I can't afford to give you a cheque that size.'

After spending the next half an hour trying to give a good description of him, using mainly four-letter words, we parted company. His behaviour probably came from having inherited a lot of money when he turned twenty-one, never having to watch his pennies. He always thought that his success was due to his own efforts, which of course was an illusion. After I'd left him, he completely mismanaged his cattle stud, leaving the valuable stud animals to die in the paddocks, too lazy to drench and spray for parasites. Justice, however, caught up with him. When I came back from an overseas trip many years later, my wife showed me a newspaper she'd been saving. In it was the great Greg, having received a prison sentence for unlawfully using the trucks on the stations he managed for carting cattle and putting the money in his own pocket.

When I worked for him, it soon became apparent he could produce any bloodline of cattle required. It's called falsifying the stud books. We fell out long before he cheated me on my commission when I found out that a cow that had been dead for years was still having calves registered. I had a very good reputation in the breeding circles, and many potential buyers would ask my advice, but it was time for me to look for greener pastures.

There was a ray of sunshine in my life with the arrival of my daughter, Anne-Britt, in December 1971. Her entry into the world wasn't smooth, and Barbara and I had a bumpy ride into parenthood. Anne-Britt was born with a faulty valve in her heart and underwent a corrective operation a few months before her second birthday to ensure she would grow up strong and healthy.

My marriage was very rocky by this stage, so a few months after Anne-Britt's surgery, I took my girls to Sweden for a well-earned break, hoping to improve our relationship. As it turned out, we only shifted our unhappiness to another part of the world. It might have worked if I had been more secure in my marriage. The emotions that overcame me when we landed in Sweden were so strong that I struggled to control them. Here I was, together with all my friends, and I neglected my family. I was meeting all the people that had made my life so wonderful again, reliving my past while forgetting I had a wife and a daughter. It would have been hard for my wife; she didn't speak any Swedish, and we stayed in the countryside most of the time. We did get a car over there, but I used it for work most of the time.

This was my first visit to Sweden in thirteen years. This stay was supposed to be a well-earned break from work and a time of

## Chapter 9: Living on the Road

bonding for my wife and me. It was a complete disaster. I didn't know how to relax and, after being asked to help cut timber after my brother's father-in-law had an accident, my brother and I worked very hard to get all the timber cut before I went back to Australia.

We had a big scare with Anne-Britt during that trip. We were handed a letter by the specialist in Perth to show doctors in Sweden in case she became even slightly sick. She was to be treated with a special drug that would stamp out any infections or other ailments. She contracted pneumonia, and with only one heart chamber working at full capacity, it was very serious.

The health service in Sweden at that time was terrible. You couldn't roll up to a hospital, no matter how sick you were, without a referral from your district nurse. When we got there, the young doctor we saw took no notice of our specialist's letter. He didn't agree that a child of her age should have such strong drugs and sent us home with what was no more than mild painkillers. Our daughter became very sick in just a few days, and I rang the hospital to tell them that we were coming straight in. 'You can't,' I was told. 'You're to have a referral from the district nurse first.'

'You will see this child without a referral or find yourself on the front page of every newspaper in this country,' I told them.

We were seen immediately and by a proper doctor. 'This child has been sick for a while,' he said. 'Why wait so long to seek help?'

When I told him about the attitude of the young doctor we'd seen the week before, he apologised, saying it should not have happened. 'Anyhow, you live in Australia now, ' he said. 'What makes that country better than ours?'

'Well, the health service for a start!' I said.

He looked at me with quite some compassion. 'I'm so sorry I wasn't here when you came in last week,' he said.

It was a shock to me to see the pitiful standard of service. In Australia, I was used to being seen quite often on the same day you made a booking. This was one of the many reasons I left Sweden; the mind-boggling inefficiency of the bureaucracy, but I think that Australian bureaucrats have beaten them by now.

Once Anne-Britt was on the mend, Olle approached me. He was cutting a big lot of timber with his father in law, who had broken his leg, and they pleaded with me to help out. Even if I hadn't been working, my wife was not keen on driving in a foreign country on the wrong side of the road. I hadn't realised how much I'd missed my earlier life; I'd always been flat out working on hacking a farm out of the scrub, but coming back to Sweden brought it back like a tidal wave. My teenage sweetheart was also constantly in my thoughts, so much so that I was too scared to ask about her. It's only now that I realise how much my friends understood; nobody offered any news about her.

Before we went on our trip to Sweden, we'd bought a large number of steers since we had a lot of good pasture. They were in a lean condition—worth about $110.00 per head—and our idea was that they would be fat and ready to sell when we came back from our trip. They were, and the first load of about forty animals made $150.00 to 160.00 per head. This was one of my better deals. In early 1974, the price of beef collapsed, and in a few weeks, the same animals were worth $35.00 per head. The price in the butcher shop never changed.

Within a week of coming back from Sweden, I had some terrible news, my second youngest sister, Lillian, had been killed in a traffic accident. Born in 1951, she had been just a toddler when I left home for my first job as a farmhand and only ten years old when I emigrated to Australia. I have fond memories of Lillian sitting on my lap and eating wild strawberries that I had picked for her. She'd had some terrible personal experiences in her life and was very shy as a result. However we caught up, it was as if one big hug from me fixed it all, and the love between us came surging back. She was in an unhealthy relationship, and the last time I saw her, we agreed it would be a good thing for her to leave the drunkard she was living with, who was also the father of her child, and come to Australia. This made her loss so much worse.

\*

I had a very large deep freeze and used to kill a big steer every Thursday or Friday, hang it from a tree branch for a day or two, and then my wife and I would spend all weekend cutting it up, putting the meat into one-kilo packs before being put in the freezer. Some animals would weigh up to 400 kilograms, and despite covering the whole kitchen floor in newspapers, there would be lots of blood and pieces of meat on it. The man on the land is constantly fighting a losing battle, yet this trend of feast or famine is mainly the fault of badly organised Aussie farmers. This came about mainly because of distance and lack of communication. Back in those days, it was very hard for the man on the land to keep himself informed of what was going on. In Sweden, for instance, at the time of my departure in 1961, fifty or more years ago, the farmers owned most of the farm produce outlets, like meatworks, sawmills, milk factories, and grain export. Payments were similar to how the grain growers of Australia were getting paid, and the businesses handling your produce keep some of the money. In a good year, this would amount to a substantial amount of money. If the next season's prices were lower, it would be propped up from this pool. This gave farmers a more even income. As a farmer myself in this country, I've experienced very high prices for sheep and wool one year, followed by rock bottom prices the next. I can remember killing sheep in the paddock and letting the pigs eat them, they wouldn't eat the wool, so we would pick that up later.

Coping with this type of unexpected loss put a lot of strain on any relationship. I moved on to leasing some very fertile land from my wife's uncle. He had been growing potatoes on some of it but was now retired. He agreed to sell the land to me, and I got busy getting a potato grower's licence. I'd become a workaholic and spent more time on the land than I did at home. My wife and I struggled for a few more years until I came home from work to an empty house one day. I don't blame her, but you would have thought that after all the unhappy time together, there might have been relief, but no. Instead, there was utter desolation: your brain doesn't take it in, and it's hard to make sense of anything. It's hard to think logically, and there is a lot of blame and bitterness. These emotions are just for us adults; what about the poor kids? There is a common belief that children have this amazing ability to adjust to virtually any situation: I'm very much opposed to this view. There have been many regrets over the years, especially in the fact we couldn't work out a better deal for the kids. In those days, the Family Court automatically declared many fathers involved in custody claims as unsuitable custodians. In one instance, I did not see Anne-Britt or my son Richard, who was born in 1976, for three months. Richard would have only just started school, and I complained to the Family Court that my children had attended six different schools in seven months. The judge informed me that travelling broadens your outlook. My barrister made the observation based on that information, His Worship had obviously never been out of his woodshed. There's no doubt in my mind that had I had my extended Swedish family close, steering me in the right direction, I would have been a much better family man. It's quite amazing how much clearer everything seems all these years later.

*

Potato farming was a constant struggle, not only against the elements, but against what was, in my opinion, the corruption in the marketing board. In WA, you have to be licenced to grow potatoes and have to sell them through a marketing board. I believe those people would have put any mafia to shame! I read an article in a Queensland newspaper in 2020 about the excessive power of the Potato Marketing Board and Agricultural Department in WA. It did not surprise me at all. My opinions have also been shaped by my personal experience and those of WA growers I have known. The regulations governing the spuds' quality was so ridiculous that it made it possible for the management to downgrade your produce whenever they wanted. Marketing wasn't completed according to the demand of the consumer and condition of the produce, but to a prewritten standard set by the Agriculture Department. The stupidity of this would be revealed later. There were other practices engaged in by the Agriculture Department that were allegedly nothing short of criminal and always using the farmers as guinea pigs. One year, we were told that the very popular variety, Sebago, was no longer up to the high standard that the Department demanded, and we had to bring in new seed potatoes. Everyone who grew certified crops had to use certified seed potatoes. The seed the

Department supplied to us was allegedly brought in from the Atherton Tableland in Queensland. Only recently, having had some dealings with the Queensland Agricultural Department, did I find out that there has never been such a thing as certified potatoes grown in Queensland and still isn't.

When I was growing certified seed, the Agricultural Department condemned my whole crop because I had mixed varieties planted on a corner of the paddock by mistake. I had forgotten to tell the two girls, later to become my stepdaughters, who were cutting potatoes for planting and put the cut one in a different stack, to start another stack when they started on a new variety. Therefore a few bags of different potatoes were mixed, but they were all of the certified seed potatoes. The Agricultural Department inspectors never spotted the patch despite several inspections. The different strains of potatoes have quite different leaves, and some have different coloured flowers. Half my crop were red-skinned potatoes, which would make it impossible, even for a highly qualified government inspector, to get them mixed up. To make it easy for them, I marked the area out and offered to sell that lot for consumption; I didn't want to take the risk of the seed crop becoming contaminated. I had a good name in the industry and liked to look after my customers, but the department head hung up on me when I pleaded with him to use common sense.

I knew a minister in the WA Government, and he asked the Minister for Agriculture to intervene. A week later, I received a letter from the man who had hung up on me with advice to mark the area in dispute and sell the spuds for consumption. Growers I'd been supplying for years told me they had lost five to six tons of production per acre using seed from my place, produced from the imported Queensland potato seed. From what I had heard,

## Chapter 9: Living on the Road

black marketing was rife since the pilfering in the board store forced the growers to sell some of their produce for cash just to keep their head above water.

I can remember one such instance when we had a very good growing season, and my crop grew a high percentage of large potatoes. At a growers' meeting in Albany, I asked the board manager if he could find a market for them, a job he was getting a lot of money to perform. 'Not a chance,' he said. 'There is no market for that size of spuds.'

'Never mind,' I told him. 'Forget about them.'

'What are you going to do about them?' he asked.

'None of your bloody business unless you're getting off your arse to sell them!'

'If you get caught selling them on the black market, you'll lose your licence,' he told me.

Well, I did sell them for cash, and I didn't get caught. The man who bought fourteen tons of them paid fifty per cent more than the board was paying for what they considered first-grade potatoes. According to them, the big spuds were considered second grade. After successfully transferring the lot to his shed, I asked how he could be happy to pay so much: $12.00 per bag whilst the board paid $8.00 per bag for first grade. His answer stunned me. 'When I order large potatoes for my fish and chip business, the board charge me $25.00 per bag because they're a special line,' he told me. The Potato Marketing Board in WA had disbanded years ago!

When I delivered large potatoes to the marketing board, I was paid $5.00 per bag since they were considered substandard. This rip off was well known, and after looking at our situation from every angle, we, the growers, decided that we would have to be less reliant on the marketing board to survive. Around that time, a fish canning factory was closing down in Albany, and several growers decided to buy it. It would be of great advantage to us since it had cold storage facilities, enabling us to store our seed potatoes between growing seasons. We could also use the factory for processing a range of products, including french fries, sweet corn, baby carrots, and beans. I spent the best part of a year trying to convince the local growers to try these crops out: there was no grower's licence required.

Having paid full interest on the loans required to get this business up and going, we were doing all right, though we were a thorn in the side of a big multinational canning factory based in Manjimup. This was in the then Minister for Agriculture's electorate. That company was granted millions of dollars to upgrade their business and spent it to undercut our prices. In a couple of years, we went broke. Not only did the multinationals get an enormous amount of money as loans from the government, but they also got it at roughly half the interest we were paying. This is one reason why the man on the land is having such a hard time, in my opinion; our governments are too busy pandering to big business to give a stuff about the small guys.

When there are concerns raised about our plight, the common cop-out is that we're unable to compete because of the subsidy paid to farmers overseas. I've farmed in Sweden and Australia, most Swedish outlets of agriculture production were owned or controlled by farmers.

Back to the marketing in WA, too many growers were bending over backwards to please the management. We put up a motion of no confidence in the board to get something done about it, but the people entrusted with presenting it to them chickened out. Working for very little return and having my produce stolen from under my nose didn't go down too well with me.

## Chapter 9: Living on the Road

I managed on my own for a while, hiring women to come in and clean the place up when it got too much. A good friend of mine who lived next door called in on me one day. With him was a beautiful woman, a good friend of his. She grew up in England and became a nurse working in the armed forces all over the world. We met at a couple of parties and enjoyed each other's company. Andy was a very well-educated lady and had a very quick wit to boost. She was into the more refined things in life and very well-read. She meant a lot to my mental nourishment, and I gained a lot from her. One thing we had in common was that we were both graduates from the hard school of life.

Andy had been deserted by her husband and was living in Albany, while I had the use of a three-bedroom cottage free of charge, not far from where my farm was situated. Andy had a young daughter going to school, but since the school bus was going past the cottage and it would mean quite a saving for both of us, they moved into my place. Shortly after, I got the finances to build a house, and things started to look up. We were married, and I felt peace once more.

Andy was a qualified nurse but was game to tackle anything life, or I dished up. One year I went over to Sweden for a month; my Dad was eighty,1986 and I had a free ticket from my ex-farming partner, Charlie's Mum and an invitation to visit her. My dear friend Charlie, a tiger for work, had a drinking problem, which worsened after I got married and we parted ways. His lawyer contacted me years later and told me he had died by suicide. Since no one in his family spoke English, I was asked if I'd be willing to act on his family's behalf to save them money for a translator. After sorting his inheritance out—all of it went to his mum—I got an invitation to visit her in Sweden, all expenses paid. She wanted to know a bit about her son's life as he hadn't written to her for many years.

I realise today how lonely Charlie must've felt at times, especially with a belly full of grog, no relations out here, and living on his own most of the time. He was not a person who got involved in the community and did not improve his English much. He did sponsor a woman from Sweden with a young daughter, but being a sailor for many years, he only knew the type of women sailors encounter when in port and didn't understand her needs.

I can't recall the woman's name or her daughters. It was such a long time ago. Still, I do remember she was a very cultured lady willing to give it Australia a go, though she'd been running a shoe shop in Sweden and got a nasty surprise when she was put to work dressing flyblown sheep the first day on the farm. There were no toilet facilities, and she was told to stick her backside over a fallen tree trunk. She came across the woods one day and approached me to ask if I could help her to get away from Charlie. I still had some contact with the boss at the meatworks in Albany and asked him to put her on. He did, but when I called in sometime later, she'd left. 'No hard feelings,' the foreman said. 'She got offered a job running a shoe shop in town, good luck to her!'

That marvellous generosity again! Being a city girl, the life proved too much for her, and she went back home. I would like to stress that her experience was not isolated. Many foreign girls who had come to Australia hoping for a better life knew nothing about the men they were meeting, only what they been told by the introduction services, and were terribly abused. With no family out here to fall back on, some committed suicide.

The money from Charlie was used up by his sisters and their husbands on holidays. Before he killed himself, he had sold his

## Chapter 9: Living on the Road

farm to a local. That farmer had bought it on a small deposit, with the rest to be paid over ten years. However, the taxation department in Sweden wanted the death duty paid on the total value of the farm. It was more than the money his mum was to receive. I arranged for his family to visit Australia many times, booking the tickets from here. They even went to America once. By the time they finished travelling, there was no money left for the Swedish tax department. It gave me a warm feeling, having cheated the tax department of that money. I knew how hard Charlie had worked for it, and it was only right that his family should get some enjoyment out of it. The terrible experience of the tax department collecting Dad's only horse all those years ago was also fresh in my memory.

While I was off to Sweden to visit with Charlie's Mum, Andy stayed on the farm. We had a lot of pigs and couldn't find someone suitable to look after them. It would have been very hard work, but she never hesitated. We worked well together, and young Claire, her daughter, was also a real tiger when it came to working. I have to say, though, I had a lot of help from her siblings as well, but they lived in Albany, a town about forty kilometres away. Once, when her Mum was overseas, we built a big storage shed together; Claire was working the forklift and me on the roof. She grew up to be a stunning looking girl; it was not long before there was a well-worn path to our humble home. She got herself a boyfriend and moved to Albany. Then there were two.

Claire's absence left a big vacuum when she moved to Albany, and it also meant there was no free help a lot of times. A terrible tragedy struck our family when we lost Claire's youngest brother, Marc. He was living in Albany but used to visit quite often. Marc was very close to Anne-Britt and Richard. Sometimes when my kids were with me on the farm, if Andy or I were late in for tea, Marc would have showered and fed them if he happened to be visiting. His death was another terrible blow to an already fragile family relationship. We'd been struggling financially. Our crops flooded a couple of times and our produce pilfered at the Marketing Board's store. The only way that I could deal with all the hardship was by shutting everyone out. My wife tried hard to engage me in talk, but it was no good. I drove her away by being so miserable. Everything but the task at hand took second place.

It wasn't as if I'd set out to make her unhappy; I didn't know how to make her happy. In hindsight, I'm starting to understand how much the hardship of hacking out a farm from the bush had affected me. What was accepted as normal by the locals, such as working in shearing sheds, eventually becoming a shearer, and saving enough money to get their block of land, was an enormous change to the world I had lived in before I came to this country. Being constantly short of money added to an increasingly unhappy marriage, and Andy left after being very unhappy for a long time. This time, thank God, there were no young kids, not that Andy's kids wouldn't have been hurting, but I hope that they realised like I did, that maybe we had all expected too much. Building something from damaged material and expecting a perfect outcome would have to be born from the belief of a 'never say die optimist' or that of a complete fool. Reluctantly, I admit that I may qualify as both. Andy now lives in WA, and we remain in regular contact. I visited her a couple of years ago and also rekindled my friendship with Claire during that visit. It means a lot to me, even though the physical distance between us is so great.

I regret very much that I didn't get to know my in-laws in England better. Andy's Dad had been a policeman all his life, and, as was the custom in those days, his wife took care of the

## Chapter 9: Living on the Road

house. He was old enough to remember the first aeroplane taking off into the air and the first man walking on the moon. They made me feel very welcome, and my mother-in-law had a wicked sense of humour. When my wife rang home and told her family that she was marrying a Swede, her Mum apparently said, 'The only thing I know about Swedes is that they're either suicidal or absolute sex maniacs.'

My wife had replied, 'Don't worry, Mum, this one is not suicidal.'

England is a beautiful country, and the people are very polite. They put a very high value on historical things rather than the 'knock it down' mentality that I feel this country suffers from. The old towns and villages are too small for traffic signals, so they just paint little roundabouts in the intersections. The rules are, of course, the same as for built ones. Their humour is unreal. I spotted some very big runner beans in a shop one day, I wanted to take some with me back to Australia since I grow a lot of vegetables, but there was no seed available. My brother-in-law offered to take me to a seed merchant he knew of, but he didn't have any seed on hand, offering to have some when I came through in a couple of weeks.

When I called in to pick them up, he looked at me with a funny expression on his face. 'May I be so bold as to ask what you're going to do with them?' he asked.

'I'm going to grow them, of course,' I said. 'What are you doing with them here in England?'

'We grow them too, of course, but that is a completely different situation. They won't grow where you're going: you're upside down to us!'

I was starting to enjoy the English humour very much by now and kept a straight face. 'It's interesting you should say that you know. I planted some seed from over here years ago but didn't have much luck. I solved the problem, though.'

'Might I ask how?' asked the seed merchant.

'You plant the seed upside down!' I explained.

The old gentleman looked at me with a blank face, 'That is absolutely brilliant,' he said. He came around the counter, 'May I shake your hand, sir, he asked. 'I never shook hands with a genius before.'

My brother-in-law is a very clever man, but not all that hot on crazy people. He looked at us as though we should both be certified and locked up.

My sister-in-law, Wendy, took us around to a lot of interesting places and I enjoyed her company very much. She has a wicked sense of humour and is a fantastic mimic; she can impersonate anyone to perfection. The agriculture would be as old as that in Sweden and has been cultivated for over 3000 years. It's possible that seed travelled backwards and forwards during the Vikings' heyday and oats were the earliest variety, mostly the wild type. One can understand why the Brits fought so hard to keep their country during the Second World War; it is truly a beautiful place.

The trip to Sweden came to an end, and we were back to much work and no money. The day came when enough was enough, and my wife left me to enjoy all that fresh air on my own. It started to dawn on me what I had lost, and I decided that farming on my own was no longer an option. After a lot of wheeling and dealing, I managed to sell the potato growing licence and the machinery and lease my farm to Colin Ayers and Sons. Now I was free to go and try something new.

CHAPTER 10

# My Gold Rush

My brother-in-law Larry, my first wife's brother, and I worked a lot together and got on well. This was, at times, the only way farmers in general survived. Larry had inherited his father's cleverness with machinery and was bloody good company. We bought a boat together so that we could go fishing and used to launch it from the beach below my farm. He offered to keep an eye on the place in my absence, and together with Les Walsh and his wife Beryl, I knew the place was in safe hands. The next morning I was ready to go.

There was a lot of gas drilling exploration up north at Barrow Island, approximately fifty kilometres northwest off the Pilbara coast of Western Australia, and I decided to give it a go. I had some very good friends living up north in Jim and Karen Kerr, and this is where I went when I left my farm. These wonderful people took me in while I went to different companies to apply for a job. However, I hadn't taken the dozens of different trade unions into account, and before I could even fill an application form in, I was required to pay union fees to every relevant union. You had to have a pretty healthy bank account to afford to apply.

In those days, the unions held the country to ransom: if you upset them, they would shut any operation down. I remember once when a big mine was closed because a plumber had replaced a broken toilet seat while doing some plumbing work. Apparently, that was a carpenter's job: it was utter madness!

As enjoyable as my stay with my friends was, even though I fished every day and never went home empty-handed, it was getting boring for a man who worked sixteen-hour days when on the farm. Thankfully, one day there was a phone call from Andy, who advised me to ring a friend of Tom Knight's who had a job available. Tom was the friend who had my problem with the Agriculture Department sorted during my potato farming days, and we used to belong to the same Lions Club.

Through Tom's connections, I found a job at Marvel Loch working with Michael 'Mike' Pietch. By the time I got to the area where the mine was, it was getting late, and Michael had asked me to call in at Southern Cross, where he lived, to get directions.

Since it was so late, his sister-in-law, Nicky, offered to come with me to the mining camp to make sure that I got a bed for the night. What a generous offer! This was a drive of some thirty kilometres at ten o'clock after a hard day's work. Nicky worked at the mine as well. I came to appreciate that side of her nature very much, and she became one of my most valued friends and a member of my shot firing crew. Together with a Kiwi by the name of Neil, Nicky and I became a very close-knit little family. She lived with her sister and Michael in Southern Cross and did a lot of running around for anybody who needed something urgently and couldn't get into town. We kept in touch for several years after I left the mining scene, but I eventually lost contact with them.

Mike was a fantastic boss, and before we broke up at Christmas, he invited the whole drill and blast team to a hotel in

## Chapter 10: My Gold Rush

town for dinner. Myself, Nicky, Neil, and Terry, our mechanic, thought we should buy him a nice bottle of wine. After talking to Tom Knight, who was working and staying at the mine he owned together with Mike, I purchased a bottle of very good port on a trip to Albany. However, when I asked around amongst the drill crew who never missed an evening when Mike was buying the beer, I found many stingy bastards. 'What are you up to? Sucking up to the boss?' was the common question when I asked for a few dollars towards the cost of the wine. I told them, 'Get stuffed! And if you turn up at the free Christmas dinner, I'll produce the present and a card with the name of the people who paid for it.'

It turned out to be a very cheap night for Mike, and the next day his wife came out and helped me wire up an area to be blasted, a job she used to do when they first started up. Nicky was a very competent person and had trained up to get a shot firer's permit. She was in charge of the biggest blast we had at that mine, of around 1400 holes and thirteen tonnes of explosives.

While working at Marvel Loch; my niece Tina wrote to me from Sweden wondering if there was a chance for a job at the mine. She was backpacking around the world and, like most backpackers, needed to work to pay for her travel expenses. There was a nice English lady named June in charge of the laboratory, where all the assaying of the gold was done, and she promised to put her on. A dozen girls were working in the lab, so Tina was in good company. I got a phone call the same afternoon she arrived and left for Perth as soon as my shift finished. I had met a young couple in Perth not long before and rang them to pick Tina up at the airport. The mine was 600 kilometres away from Perth, and I hadn't been able to get the next morning off at such short notice, so I had to get back that night. It was a round trip of 1200 kilometres! Tina told me stories and sang to keep me awake. I think it was two in the morning when we got back to the mine, and breakfast was at seven. It was a hell of a long day.

I recall one day at Marvel Loch in WA, when we were blasting a lot of old diggings, and an older man stopped at a roadblock that I was manning; we had to stop all traffic on the road going through the site, as there was danger from flying rocks when the blast went off. This old man put his head out the window and said, 'It looks like you're blasting the South Bronco pit.'

'That's correct mate, what do you know about it?'

'I used to work underground there many years ago. Keep your eyes open; you might find my old hard hat,' he said.

It turned out that he'd been working there about sixty to seventy years earlier. We never found his hat, of course, but there were a lot of empty bottles and tins, and today, you see them all along the roadsides.

It may not seem like a very interesting job, blasting dirt, but I had never done anything so fascinating in my life before. This area, in particular, came up with various types of ore at every blast. It was broken ground with lots of small tunnels and cavities, filled with water and little gemstones, but it also had a lot of sulphuric gas trapped underground, and we required gas masks when drilling at night. During the day, the toxic gases would escape the pit as the air warmed up. Sulphuric gas is very hot and very damaging, not only for people but also for the engines in the drill rigs we used. The same engine that would last ten thousand hours back on the farm was worn out in a couple of thousand hours in the mine. I remember one day when we'd primed a large area to be blasted. This involved putting all the initiating explosives down the drill holes and then putting rolled up, empty plastic bags in the holes to stop anything falling in and blocking them while we went to the mess for lunch. We came back to load

## Chapter 10: My Gold Rush

the main explosives into the holes and found a lot of the bags and fuses had melted. It would have been hot enough to cook eggs.

This was a very rich mine, but because of the minerals in the ground beside gold, graphite being one of them, a large heap of gold-bearing ore was stacked on top of the ground: the gold just couldn't be extracted from it. I ran into the former manager of the mine years later, and he told me it was still there inside security fencing, having lime irrigated through it to change the acidity level. It was thought that it would be possible to extract the gold once the ph level was high enough. Eventually, as happens so often in the gold mining industry, the company went broke and we were all sent home.

I went back to check on my farm, but within days, Mike rang up and told me he wanted me to take charge of a contract blasting job in a pretty isolated area. 'Go to the depot and pick a good four-wheel drive and the best man in the crew,' he said.

'I'll take Tom Waters,' I said.

'He is illiterate,' said Mike.

'Yes, I know,' I said, 'but I don't think we'll be spending much time in the library.'

'Right. You know what you're doing. Get up there as soon as possible.'

We went across the country where some early explorers had been bogged down with their camel teams. It took us a full day to get across those vast salt flats, where those camels got bogged. The surface looked hard and dry, but in patches, there was brine underneath. Those poor animals would have cut the skin on their legs breaking through the hard crust and be quite lame from the salt eating into them.

Tom had been doing some potato picking on my farm many years before, and when a friend of his brought him to the drilling company where I was in charge, I thought he looked familiar. 'Have I seen you before? I asked. 'Have you been doing any work out around Bornholm, picking potatoes perhaps?'

'No,' he said. 'That's a mug's game. I did it once for some Russian farmer at Bornholm, he was a hard bastard to please, and I never tried it again.'

'He was not Russian. It was me!'

I said, 'I thought I remembered you.'

The poor man went pale. He badly wanted a job. 'No, no, it wasn't you, ' he said. 'Anybody can see you're a good guy!'

'If I remember right, you were a bloody hard worker, Tom, ' I said. 'You can start right away.'

His face lit up, 'You won't regret it, Bill, I promise!'

He was a very hard and honest worker, and that's why I picked him to come with me on this job. He could be quite funny at times, and we worked at a hell of a pace. One day when I told him to hurry up, he turned on me and said, 'Pray that you don't have an accident: you would need an oil transfusion. You're not human, you bastard!'

He is one of the few men who has been able to keep up with me. Tom was Irish, and one of those kids the church had abused. He was dyslexic, and the good Christian brothers told him he was not worth spending the time on educating. 'They worked us harder than if we'd been animals,' he said. 'There wouldn't have been a day you didn't get a big work boot up your arse. If that was all that was rammed up your backside, it was a good day.'

He had me in tears.

While working with Hardrill, I found there were some interesting characters around. One such wonder turned up at the mess one morning, introducing himself as 'crazy' and wanted a job. I'd never hired anyone on a recommendation like that before

## Chapter 10: My Gold Rush

but found out that 'Crazy' was his nickname. However, there had been a slight spelling mistake, and it should have read 'Lazy'. I'd never met anyone before who could apply so little strain to his body or remain motionless for such a length of time without falling over or going to sleep.

He came back from a long weekend off, Easter, I think, telling us how drunk he'd been, which was the main topic of conversation in a mining camp. In those days, you were allowed to stay in the pub until you'd finished the drinks you had on the table at closing time. The dedicated drinkers used to order in jugs of beer and had one hour—the swilling hour—to get rid of them before closing. As Crazy told the story, they had ordered in a dozen jugs, and during that final hour, they were half price. 'We managed to drink them all before closing time,' he said, 'but was I hangover the following day. I thought I would die.'

In our crew was a farmer boy from Esperance, a quiet, slow-talking man, who said, 'Well, you might have been sick, Crazy, but at half price, think of all that money you saved. If you had been on long service leave and kept drinking, you might have been able to retire on your savings.'

Crazy looked as if he had missed a big opportunity. Remarks like that are a lot funnier than any so-called stand-up comedian quips, and there were many of them during my time in the mining industry.

Many people in the mining industry have nothing saved, despite years of very high wages. A lot of them simply have various level of brain damage through the misuse of drugs and alcohol. One I remember was a real slob who resented me coming to work every day clean and tidy. One day at breakfast, he looked across at me from the opposite side of the table and said, 'Do you realise, Bill, that you've got your hair parted differently this morning?'

I took his hand in mine, 'I'm so happy that you noticed,' I said. 'I didn't think that you cared.'

He pulled his hand back as if he been burnt. He looked around the table, 'I'm not like that,' he said. 'I swear I don't know what this weird bastard is on about.'

He never worried me again.

During one of the slack days at the mine where we were contract blasting, we took a drive to a big mine some thirty kilometres away to see if they did things differently. A buxom redhead, known as Big Red, offered to take us for an inspection tour of the mine site upon our arrival. As we followed her into the office building after our tour, I ran into my next-door neighbour, Rolf Gutlich. He was the surveyor at this mine. He invited us home for a cuppa and told me that the management at this mine was looking for a reliable shot firer at an outlying mine. After contacting the superintendent, I was told to come over and have a chat. I told Rolf it would have to be very early in the morning since we were very busy at the mine I was currently employed at. 'Alright with me,' he said.

At half-past five the next morning, I met with Gary Zuvich, the superintendent at that mine, and it was agreed I would start there as soon as my current employers had found a replacement. This was most unusual since the common practice was to disappear during the night once you had a job lined up. 'The fact that you asked for a week stay says a lot about you. That's the sort of people I want on my team,' he said.

When I told my current boss about my intention to start a new job, he was very understanding: 'I can understand that you want to advance to better things, we got a young bloke here that got a blasting licence, but I don't think he's done any, you better give him a crash course.'

## Chapter 10: My Gold Rush

It made me feel very pleased that he was so good about it, and when the week was up, I moved to Reedy's, the new gold mine. The superintendent who had employed me was a big man of Yugoslav background, highly competent and very fair in all the dealings I had with him: 'You run the blasting and drilling, and you answer to me. If there is anything that I can do to help, just ask.'

There were many times I made use of his offer.

Not only were the days busy, but after I'd been back to the mess for tea, I'd go back to the pit to organize the night shift. Sometimes Big Gary, the superintendent, would set up the floodlights for me. He was a pleasure to work with, and I felt a lot of satisfaction in my job. There was, however, a lot of rumbling among the crew. They had been used to getting away with murder: drinking all night, neglecting the machinery—most of which was very expensive—and when caught out, they'd buy their leading hand or foreman beer all night to get off the hook. It didn't work with me. I came from a country where the capacity of your brain was valued more than the capacity of your bladder. I was getting a reputation for getting things done, having lifted production considerably since my arrival, and I wasn't going to have some lazy slackers sabotaging my work and reputation.

Gary appreciated my effort to smarten the men up. He had told me on arrival that any hiring and firing was to be done by him only, but after a while, he gave me more or less a free hand. Being able to choose the men who were willing to put in a day's honest work in return for very high wages resulted in a crew that was the envy of the surrounding mines. A lot of those men came from my area of the state, and most of them were working at sawmills when I got in touch with them. Working in hardwood mills is very taxing with little reward. In comparison, operating an air-conditioned drill rig for three times the money made them feel like they were in heaven. Gary said that he wished he had the same result at his mine, the one where I'd run into my neighbour.

Now that I'm getting on a bit in age, I realise that had I experienced the same with personnel management earlier in life, there would have been many more happy people around, including myself. Somebody must have been keeping an eye on me because one day, when I went into the next town some thirty kilometres away to pick up supplies for the drill crew, I ran into the manager of the supply business, Henning. He was a Danish man. We became very good friends, and having another family next door was a joy. We used to get all our consumables for our rigs from Perth, 1000 kilometres away. We worked out a deal that left Henning supplying all of those consumables, which meant that instead of waiting, at times, several days for parts, I could pick them up from him and be back in a couple of hours. Sometimes, Lorraine, his wife, would have made a cake when I arrived if she was given a bit of warning. Being stuck so far from civilization is pretty hard, but having this marvellous couple next door made it quite enjoyable.

Andy lived in Perth at that time, and even though we were separated, she came up for a few days and Lorraine organized a party. Some party! There was a lot of vodka in the deep freeze and a lot of helpers to get rid of it. Every time we toasted each other, someone had to say something clever. By the time the bottle had been around the table five or six times, everyone was a genius. There were quite a number of nationalities, and it was marvellous to hear the same songs in everyone's own language, in unison.

The company I worked for was very generous to its workforce, providing motel style accommodation and top-class tucker.

## Chapter 10: My Gold Rush

One morning, as I came into the mess for breakfast, there was a new cook: a beautiful blonde woman by the name of Karen. As it turned out, she was as far away from home as I was, all the way from England and working her way around the world. This would have been like solitary confinement for a girl like her. We began talking in the leisure room one day, and it turned out we were both keen on playing Scrabble. She was sick of having nothing to do after work except drink and play darts in the wet mess. We became very good friends and used to play every Saturday evening. She was like family to me and would often borrow my car when she had to go to town shopping. She even bought Christmas presents for me and was a truly sweet person whose company I enjoyed. Only people who have lived in remote camps with several hundred men whose collective interest was to get blotto every night (because as in Crazy's case, the beer is only half price) can understand how much a civilized and intelligent person like Karen was appreciated by those of us with other interests. I will come back to her later.

A big change took place in my life not long after Karen started as a breakfast cook. Gary had to go back to a permanent position at the mine where my neighbour was a surveyor, and a new superintendent was employed to replace him: everything took a turn for the worst, and it was clear this new man was a complete dickhead. He had previously been in charge at an iron ore mine in WA and knew nothing about gold mining. To cover up his inability, he'd go around and change some of the work practices which had taken me the better part of a year to implement. He was a walking disaster, and we were constantly at odds.

After a few months, he told me one day that I was having a week off. 'You work too hard,' he said.

'Can't be done,' was my reply. 'We've opened up a couple more pits, and I can't see how you're going to cope without me.'

'You are having a week off!'

That was the end of our discussion. On my return from Perth, I went down into the pit to find the young man who had been working under me, learning to blast so he could sit for his shot firing ticket. He was studying for his pit manager's exam and needed the ticket to sit for it. He told me that Bryan, the superintendent wanted the shot pattern we were using changed. 'I've marked out the new patterns,' he said.

I told him that if the super wanted to change anything, he was to see me about it first: as far as I knew, I was still in charge. He got a bit pink around the gills. 'Have you been into your office this morning?' he asked. 'There's a letter there for you from the super.'

When I got back to my office, there was a letter informing me management had concluded my job was too much for one man. Because of my invaluable contribution, it had been decided to increase the number of shot firers to two. One of the men who had been wriggling into the super's pockets had been given my job, but they would be very happy for me to stay on as an adviser, given my experience.

What a difference it would make to the quality of the workforce if people were employed for their mental capacity rather than the capacity of their bladder. *What a gutless man!* The super had sent me on a week's break, presumably out of concern for my wellbeing, and was then too gutless to tell me about the changes when I got back. To top it off, now this miserable excuse for a man was asking me to stay to babysit the carpenter. Yes, that's who got my job.

I walked into Bill, the manager's office. I can't remember his surname, but Bill asked me to file an official complaint about

## Chapter 10: My Gold Rush

the superintendent when I told him how useless he was. The manager knew this as well as I did but was too weak to act. I told him so at the time, and it went down like a lead balloon. Bill was now gloating, 'How do you feel about your demotion?' he asked gleefully.

'Well, you can stop smiling,' I said. 'Not only have I put up with a lot of dimwits and am expected to be able to get some sort of production out of them, but now the inmates have taken over the asylum. If you think you will be happy with the situation you've created, you're kidding yourself, I wish you good luck, and I'm handing in my resignation.'

That wiped the smile off his face. The very next morning, Bill came to my cabin as I was ready to leave, all flustered and asked me if I could stay on for a couple of hours: the contractor who delivered the blasting gel into the pit had arrived, and nobody knew where to send him. Was I enjoying this? You bet!

What they hadn't realised when they'd plotted my demise was the high regard in which I was held by Gary, the guy who employed me in the first place, and the head office in Perth. I had been invited to a barbecue at the mine where he was in charge a couple of weeks earlier, and as we were chatting, he told me he never had in his life poached staff from another mine. 'I don't intend to start now, but having said that, if you should find that you can't work with the management at your mine, there's always a job here for a man like you.'

Something else happened that morning when I arrived back from my week off. Karen asked from across a couple of tables away at breakfast, 'Have you been telling any new lies lately?'

I looked at her bewildered. I had no idea what she was talking about, and some of the crew sitting at the table were averting their eyes. 'What's going on here?' I asked but got no answers.

I realised then that the gutless wonders behind the plot to get rid of me had also been busy spreading lies. That Karen, whom I trusted more than anyone else at the mine, would have believed any of them rocked me to the core. I couldn't bring myself to talk to her. I was running the drill and blast operation in five different pits at the time and putting in 16 hours a day. I could cope with the physical part of it, but realising just how far management would stoop and the fact that they were succeeding was the straw that broke the camel's back. A mental breakdown was staring me in the face, I was exhausted, and it all added up to my decision to quit.

A couple of weeks after I left, Henning, my Danish mate rang me and told me that the superintendent who had plotted my demise so successfully had been sacked. It did not surprise me. I was feeling quite good about him getting his just desserts, and yet, it was a bittersweet feeling.

CHAPTER 11

# A Mighty Fall

Andy and I went to Thailand with some friends in late 1984 to break up the monotony of life on the farm. One of my friends, James, was born in Thailand, and the trip coincided with his fiftieth birthday. We stayed in a house in Bangkok that belonged to his brother. During that time, I came to appreciate the generosity of the Thai people. We were taken everywhere sightseeing and ate the most delicious food. We travelled by train to Chiang Mai, the old Capital City, about 900 kilometres north of Bangkok. The paddy fields along the railway line were full of moving lights. Asking James what was going on, I was told it was people out catching frogs. Deep-fried frogs are a delicacy in Thailand!

For the Thais, it is safe to go fishing and grow crops on their land. In those countries bombed during the Vietnam War, however, people run the risk of getting blown up every time they enter their fields. This has brought famine to previously well-fed people, and many fields are simply too dangerous to plant or fish. I have a very dear friend from Laos who told me about her experiences from the war. Her country had food shortages because the Americans didn't care where they dropped their bombs. Despite signing an international pact stipulating Laos was to be left alone, millions of tons were dropped on her country to make sure that the Viet Cong—Vietnamese resistance fighters—had nowhere to hide. She was scavenging dustbins at hotels and restaurants for something to eat, even melon rinds. They would scrape the rinds from the inside until they got to the green outer rind. That any country involved in the Vietnam War can celebrate their involvement has never sat well with me.

The first night there, we were taken out for a meal by an old school friend of James' who had travelled there by car that day, 900 kilometres from Bangkok. He owned a longan plantation on the outskirts of the city and invited us to his home for a typical Thai meal one evening. We must have had dozens of different dishes! The meal lasted for hours, but we never felt that we'd eaten too much, as often happen when eating western food.

Having James in our group made it easier to get around because he spoke the language. His friends organized a party one night to celebrate his making it to half a century on earth. The venue was a fair way out of Bangkok, and as we walked in, we noticed some big cement blocks and planks stacked along the side of the restaurant, which I thought looked a bit untidy, but that's Bangkok. It turned out to be an unbelievable evening. Enormous amounts of food and even more drinks were consumed. James and one of his friends went downstairs to the toilet but were away for a long time, so much, so his wife asked me to go and have a look for them. 'Something must have happened to them, ' she said.

I went downstairs and outside the row of cubicles stood one of James friends. He was built like a sumo wrestler and spoke limited English. 'What you want?' he asked.

## Chapter 11: A Mighty Fall

'I came down to look for my friend,' I said.

'Why you look?' he asked.

'Because I'm worried about him,' I said.

'Around here, I worry,' said the sumo wrestler.

As I stood at the urinal, minding my own business, something warm was wrapped around my neck, and someone started to give me a massage. My hand went to my back pocket where my wallet was.

'Don't worry, sir,' someone said in perfect English. 'I work here, and my job is to make you relax. The more relaxed, the more you will pee.'

The more you pee, the more room in your bladder for more drinks. There were some smart business brains at work. As I was taking this in, a devilish thought came to me, *James was the old English school type and would not appreciate having a man giving him a massage.* I said to the fellow working on me, 'Come with me upstairs. There's a bloke there that would love a good gentle massage.'

Up we went to find James half slumped in his chair. I pointed him out to the masseur, who got his warm towel, wrapped it around James' neck and started caressing him. The result was nothing short of a miracle! James suddenly sat straight up in the chair from being out for the count, giving me a vicious stare across the table. 'Get rid of him,' he growled. The poor man gave me a puzzled look and left.

By this time, the sumo wrestler friend of James decided to give a speech. 'Dear friend,' he said. 'Long time we not see you, but anything you want, we give.'

James, normally very properly mannered, looked up with a devilish grin: 'How about a bit of 'nooky' then?' he asked.

Nooky is English slang for sex, and it was obvious the big man didn't know the term. He looked around the tables, a worried expression developing on his face. 'My friend,' he said, 'we have Mekong whisky, Tiger beer, brandy, and wine, no 'nooky'.'

He was given a standing ovation. No comedian could have produced anything so funny nor expressed it so sincerely.

The evening was coming to an end, and as we walked out of the restaurant and headed for the parking area, the purpose of the cement blocks and planks became obvious. During the time we'd been inside, there had been a heavy shower, the kind you only get in the tropics. There was about a foot of water covering the ground, and this makeshift walkway worked perfectly to keep our feet dry. However, the fellow we'd come to the restaurant with, another of James' school friends, had a problem. Having been shot during his time in the police force, he had a busted knee and limped badly. Tonight, it was even worse.

The reason was mainly that he was walking with one foot on the ramp, the other in a foot of water on the side. 'Hop in,' he said when we got to his car.

'Who is driving?' I asked. Having followed his progress during the evening with interest, I was more than a little bit worried.

'Why?' he glared at me. 'You don't think I can drive?'

His wife said something, and there was a bit of an argument, but she got in the driver's seat and off we went. Dick, the Thai guy, barked something at her, and the headlights came on; we'd been driving without them up until then. We hit a stretch of road that was flooded; another bark and the windscreen wipers started up. We got back to our house in one piece, and the next morning I commented on how lucky we'd been to have Dick's wife to take us home. Karen, James' wife, spoke up and said, 'You know, she has never driven that car before.' It was a night

## Chapter 11: A Mighty Fall

I'll never forget for so many reasons, but most of all, because they were such wonderful people and so generous.

Before we left Bangkok, we were invited to an Indian tailor's home for a traditional Indian dinner. We all had suits and dresses made by him, and this was his way of saying thank you. After dinner, we were shown slides from their wedding. It was an arranged one, and the feast lasted for a week. I asked the wife what the women thought about arranged marriages, and her answer made a lot of sense. She said there was a much better chance of a long-lasting marriage when two people from families that knew each other well tied the knot, compared with total strangers marrying. The family ties are very strong in the eastern tradition, as is their tolerance.

\*

Back at home, I found new employment at Metana Minerals in Mount Magnet and things were going along smoothly until one night when I was moving my rig into another pit that had no lights in it. There was a lighting plant on the edge of the pit that I intended to start up, but it was a pitch-black night, and the torch I had didn't work. Still, I knew where the plant was situated, or so I thought. Parking my rig and proceeding carefully towards where the plant was, I missed it and could not see any landmarks. I became completely disorientated. I started back to my rig, which I could hear running. After a few steps, the ground disappeared under my feet, and I fell into what I thought was a mine shaft. It is amazing how much goes through your mind in a fraction of time. I remember thinking that my remains would never be discovered before hitting the bottom and passing out.

When I came to, I could feel my hardhat next to me and put it back on. Feeling around me, there was nothing, though after taking a few steps, I could feel a small drill rig. I realised I had fallen into one of the pits. The situation was pretty serious; the pits are taken down in steps of fifteen metres, called 'benches' and then stepped, leaving a ledge a few metres wide before going down to the next one. It was clear to me by now what had happened, and I remembered that the drill rig I had found and missed landing on by only a few steps was parked up next to the haul road on one such bench.

That was great: just find the haul road and walk out. The problem was, I couldn't remember which side of the road it was parked on. Having just fallen fifteen metres and knocking myself out, I was very reluctant to move, but the only way to find the road was to walk along the bench until I found the haul road. Starting the walk and hanging onto the pit wall, it seemed hours before I got found it. I fell another few metres where the dirt had been excavated. When I finally made it back to the surface, my rig was still idling on the side of the pit, so I turned it off and walked down to the workshop.

The mechanic on duty got a shock when he saw me. 'Sit down, sit down!' he kept telling me. 'You need to see a doctor, don't panic.'

When we got to the hospital, the doctor who I'd seen only a few days before asked my name. When told, he said, 'I remember you, but you look different.' That was the understatement of the year! The left side of my face was collapsed, my nose was pushed to one side, and I was bleeding like a stuck pig. The mining company had its own ambulance. I was taken to a bigger hospital that night before being flown by the Flying Doctor Service to a specialist hospital in Perth.

## Chapter 11: A Mighty Fall

A year or so earlier, a man from Perth came to Reedy's when I was working there. He was on his way around Australia on a fundraising drive for the Flying Doctors. He was pushing a wheelbarrow and called into as many mine sites as was practical; he figured the people working there would have plenty of cash to part with. He was in for a surprise: those people had plenty of cash, but were not very willing to part with any of it. The same people who would think nothing of spending $50.00 on drinks in one day were only chucking small coins into his wheelbarrow. Since I didn't drink much and still had enough brain cells working, I could see both sides of humanity. Here was a man giving up a lot of his time to help his fellow man, and on the other side were a mob of beer-swilling men who couldn't care less. As it happened, I had my chequebook on me and wrote him a cheque for fifty dollars. I'm sure it would have stood out like a sore thumb among the pitiful collections of coins, but the beer swillers still just threw peanuts in. During my long stay in the hospital, I thought quite often about how lucky I was to have a service like the Flying Doctors available at the time of my accident. I appreciated, even more, the effort of the 'wheelbarrow man'.

Metana Minerals supported me after my accident and provided somewhere for me to stay in Perth while recuperating. They offered me a job at the head office, which involved checking invoices to help along with my brain function: it had been knocked about pretty badly. The office was close to my accommodation, and it was up to me what hours I worked. Whenever I felt that I'd had enough, I was free to knock off. It was a long road back to full recovery, but I was well looked after, and on my return to the mining settlement where the accident happened, the management told me to stay in the office and compile a handbook about drilling and blasting procedures.

A few months after my return, the company ceased to operate, and we were all out of a job. There was a lot of demand for drill rig operators, and I worked at several different mines on a lot of different machines, but it wasn't enough of a challenge for me. When I saw an advertisement for an operator in the Northern Territory, I applied. The man who had posted the advertisement wanted me there as soon as possible, so I went to Perth where Andy lived and informed her of my plans.

CHAPTER 12

# The Top End

Before I went to the Northern Territory, there were a few things to organize. Since a trip of that distance covered vast areas of nothing, I needed to put in a bit of planning. I spent the best part of a day getting some spare parts, like fan belts and a few other things, for the car. As I was having a cup of coffee in the city, a lanky young man sat down next to me. He worked at Reedy's as a drill operator and was a very likeable young fellow, but I had to sack him because he would readily leave his machine if someone asked him for a helping hand, resulting in no blast holes drilled. I tried to explain to him several times why he couldn't do this, but he didn't get it.

'How are you going, John?' I asked.

'I'm alright,' he said, 'what about you? Someone told me a while back that you'd had an accident, fell fifteen metres down a pit and hit the bottom head first.'

'That's more or less right,' I replied.

'Well, I hate repeating myself, but I said it then, and I'll say it again: you were very lucky. If you had come down feet first, you could have been seriously hurt.'

I appreciate that type of humour, and it probably made him feel better.

The next morning I was on my way, travelling some 1,400 kilometres on that first day alone. There are no signs of civilization once you get a few hundred kilometres north of Perth, so you put your foot to the floor and fly. It was the wettest season in memory across the Top End, and after having spent the first night in Onslow, I nearly disappeared into a deep gutter the following day, which had been cut across the highway by the floodwater. If I had continued the journey the night before, I would likely not be writing this book. The Kimberly region was an unbelievable experience. Much has been written about the Grand Canyon in America, but I think this country has its own unique and spectacular scenery. I had not seen such unbelievable scenery in real life before, only in cowboy films! Every range you came through held another surprise. I thought about the new settlers in America and South Africa, the difference being that I would see new scenery every day, whereas they would have taken weeks to see the same area. After a very brief stay in Kununurra, I travelled along the Victoria River flood plains. This was some of the best cattle country in WA where Janet Holmes à Court ruled. On a visit to Sweden, I brought with me a newspaper article, where she was described as the biggest single cattle owner in the world. At the time, she was estimated to own 750,000 head of cattle.

On my arrival at the mine site at Pine Creek the following day, I was told they were closing up and that we were moving to a different place. And we later moved to Hayes Creek. It had been mined in the early days of settlement by the Chinese and the landscape looked like swiss cheese, with holes everywhere and in between. I actually ended up blasting some of these early

## Chapter 12: The Top End

diggings in a few different places and was amazed at how anyone could have worked in such terrible conditions. The diameter of the tunnels they used for getting the ore out would not have been more than half a metre, and they had a small set of rails and trollies they pushed in front or behind them to get the ore out, some of them quite long. They depended a lot on guesswork as to where the ore body would be heading once they ran out of gold on the spot they were working. An old miner told me that a reef will always point in the direction of the compass: north to south or west to east. It might be something in this and would certainly explain why the miners kept going underground for quite a distance sometimes, losing the reef of gold and catching it again. Because of the depth underground, the temperature was very even and dry. The rail tracks had no rust on them.

Back at Hayes Creek, I filled a lot of different roles at the start, having a wide range of experience. One night, I was relieving for one of the drillers who had taken ill, and when my shift was finished, I had the drill stuck deep in the ground because of a faulty air supply on the rig. It took ages to get out, but there is an unwritten rule among drill operators; you don't leave a drill stuck in the ground for the next operator to get out. My boss, John Jeans, was a grumpy bloke with the shortest fuse known to mankind, and as I came up from the pit, he roared, 'Where the hell have you been?' And he was in a pretty good mood that morning.

Well, I was not. 'I've been stuck in a hole for hours because of a faulty airline. Your rigs are a disgrace!' I said.

'Hop in my ute. I'll take you back to camp,' John said.

*Well*, I thought, *this didn't last long.* When you were fired, you were usually taken back to camp to collect your belongings and put on the bus down in the village.

We got to the mess, and John surprised me when he asked if he could join me for a cuppa while I had my breakfast. 'So, you don't like drilling,' he said.

'I don't mind if the rigs are in good condition,' I replied.

He glared at me, 'No need to repeat yourself, I heard you the first time. How would you like to keep an eye on the workshop, make sure we got everything needed at all times and keep the drill bits sharp?'

He had a sharpening machine worth many thousands of dollars, but nobody with much of an idea on how to work it. 'I'll send you to Darwin, to a big workshop that has the same type of machine. Stay for a week and learn to master it. You will be responsible for keeping the drilling operation running smoothly by having everything needed at all times. What do you say?'

'Keep talking,' I replied. 'I have been thinking of getting my wife over here from Perth. I'll get a flat in Darwin and will be able to transport all the consumables needed for our operation here myself, but I've only got a car.'

'I'll supply a one-ton utility,' he said, 'and you can drop the orders for anything we need into the different suppliers on a Friday and pick them up first thing on Monday, on your way back to work.'

It sounded pretty good to me; at most mines, you worked two weeks straight and had one week off. With this job, I'd be home every weekend. However, I had a lot to learn about life in the Top End. The first Friday, I arrived in Darwin about lunchtime, giving me plenty of time to drop my orders in. But there was hardly any staff available anywhere to give the orders to. They had all knocked off before lunch to get the barbecue going and the beer out, and they certainly weren't going to halt their favourite pastime to deal with me. That meant I had to leave the mine site Thursday, which gave me even more time off, away from the mine.

John, my boss, was about twenty years younger than me with plenty of attitude. Surprisingly, we formed a pretty strong friendship, which lasted all the time I worked for him. One of my tasks was to supervise new drillers if they had no experience with our rigs, and many times when I returned on Monday morning, a driller had been sacked, and a new one was starting. I got to meet a lot of drill operators during my time with John.

Not long after I was settled with a flat in Darwin, I flew over to Perth and drove back with Andy. We'd been separated a number of years and had decided before I left for Darwin that if I succeeded there, we'd give our marriage another go. This was as good as it got. Andy got a job with a welfare organisation as a nurse, doing home visits and helping people out. One such family was that of the magistrate in Darwin. His wife and Andy became good friends. We had a drink with them occasionally, and a few amusing yarns were told. One was about a local man who hardly ever worked but still got by. He was a 'long grass' occupant: people who had no home but survived quite comfortably in the open because of the climate. One day, on the way back to his camp after a day of heavy drinking, he stole a new mower from a hardware store and pushed it home. When he woke up the next morning, he realised it had been a dumb thing to do since everybody knew he couldn't afford a new mower. This fellow was half-Irish, and here is an example of the famous way they think. How could he put the mower back without attracting attention? Simple! He pushed it up the street back to the store and told the storekeeper that he had found it under a bush. Could it belong to them? Yes, it did! 'We had one stolen yesterday, as a matter of fact. Thank you for being so honest and bringing it back all this way. We would like to give you a reward.'

'Think nothing of it,' said the Irishman. 'But if you insist, a carton of beer wouldn't go astray.'

The storekeeper was more than happy to fulfil his wish. A carton of beer, or multiples of, was the most common currency used in Darwin

Another time, he was in court charged with assault as he'd broken someone's nose. The magistrate asked him if he had any mitigating circumstance in his defence. 'Yes, your honour,' came the answer. 'I heard the man I hit talking about me in a very offensive manner to a group of people a short distance away. He was calling me a "silly old c**t".'

'If he didn't actually say it to your face,' said the magistrate, 'I can't accept that as a mitigating circumstance. You have to prove he was actually talking about you.'

'That's easy, your honour,' said the Irishman. 'I was the only silly old c**t there.'

The magistrate told me later, 'I tell you, Bill, it's very hard to keep a straight face in court at times.'

The lifespan of the open cut mine was coming to an end, and the operation was to continue underground. The attitude of management regarding the safety of the workforce did not instil much confidence when we worked in the open pit, and going underground didn't appeal to me, so I quit.

While learning how to operate the sharpening machine in Darwin, I'd met a bloke who owned a fishing boat. He was a good friend of the business owner where I was learning how to work the sharpening machine. Since I now had time on my hands and loved fishing, I contacted him and asked if he would employ me as a deckhand. He was on sick leave from the mine where he'd

## Chapter 12: The Top End

worked after an accident, but even though he could still manage the boat, he had no money to fuel it up. I offered to pay upfront for any start-up costs and take it out of the catch: done.

We went out for a week at a time, and it was the most carefree time of my life. After the first trip, we decided to head to a new fishing ground that had never been properly mapped. This meant there would likely be plenty of fish. We bought a GPS (Global Positioning System) and sailed into the unknown. We knew bugger all about how to operate this piece of equipment but had a lot of confidence we would learn on the way.

Coming out of the port in Darwin, I took control of the wheel while the skipper had a bit of shuteye. Imagine my surprise when I looked at our brand new navigation system screen to see us 'reversing' the boat down the coastline. What the hell was going on? Well, not knowing how to operate the system correctly, we'd forgotten to mark our new waypoint as we altered course, so the boat was still pointing to the old one—what a couple of dimwits.

There were a few close shaves where a man could have easily lost his manhood. It was a forty-foot boat but had no toilets fitted; you just had to fire over the side of the boat. One morning, as I stood up from having finished my morning toilet, a giant hammerhead shark swam past underneath the boat. It was nearly as wide as the boat. Had I still had my backside hanging over the side, I would have come home and joined the girls' choir. Another time on our way back home, I spotted a couple of seagulls surfing on the big swell that was running. They were standing up with the water just covering their feet, going up one big swell and disappearing over the crest. At that stage, we'd been out for a week in some very rough weather. It is very tiring, being constantly on the watch, so I decided not to tell the other guys just in case they thought I'd gone mad. Suddenly, the gulls came out of the water altogether: they were standing on the back of a giant turtle, of which there were plenty. She had been swimming just under the surface, and the gulls were getting a free ride.

One day, when we were busy catching what they call Golden Snapper up north and Mangrove Jack down south, now and then, we'd pull up only half of one. A shark was getting his dinner for free. We baited a large hook attached to a chain, put a fish weighing a couple of kilograms on for bait, tied it to the anchor chain, and waited. Within a few minutes, the boat started rocking violently. We'd caught a large tiger shark. We left it on there for a while until it tired itself out, got it alongside and slipped a couple of ropes under it. While the skipper and an English tourist we'd met, who had begged us to come along, held it tight up against the side of the boat, I hung over the side and cut the spine just behind the head. This serves two purposes; it immobilises the shark and drains the ammonia from the glands located there. This was a massive shark; it took the three of us all the strength we could muster to roll it in over the railing. It would have been close to 400 kilograms, and the skipper was rubbing his hand in anticipation of all the money it would bring. He spent hours cutting it up into smaller pieces for the shops. It stank of ammonia, and I didn't think anybody would buy it. When we opened the box up in a shop, the storekeeper yelled at us to get 'the bloody thing' out of his shop and, as a matter of fact, out of the city.

The skipper was a Lapp from Sweden – a term of endearment used for people from a region in the very north of Sweden with mixed bloodlines – and he had his languages mixed up a bit. Literacy was not his strong point, as it turned out. We came in fully loaded from a week of good fishing, and it was early evening. As usual, it gets dark very quickly in the tropics, and we

## Chapter 12: The Top End

were heading for the mooring where we'd anchor for the night and unload in the morning. We had a rubber dinghy aboard, which we were using to get back to shore, and that night, we only got a few metres when the outboard motor on the dinghy hit something. We couldn't find anything stuck in the propeller and started again, but a few metres later, the same thing happened. I said to Hilding, the skipper, 'We're hitting bottom!' and jumped into the water. It was only a foot deep. We walked back to shore dragging the dinghy and were probably the only fishermen in Darwin to have crossed the harbour on foot. I was bitten by something along the way, and it hurt like hell!

We had the car parked at the boat club, and after putting the dinghy in the back, we went into the club to have a few beers before going home. As we were sitting there, a couple of other fishermen came over. 'You're getting a bit reckless coming in at low tide with a full load on! It's a wonder you didn't run aground,' they said.

'What are you talking about? I checked the tidal chart before we got into the harbour,' Hilding said.

One of the men pulled out a chart, 'Take a look,' he said, 'it's low tide.'

That made sense since we'd dragged the dinghy halfway across the Darwin harbour. The skipper had been reading the tidal chart for a different month. 'Are you getting danger money?' the men asked me with big smirks on their faces.

'No,' I said, 'just free entertainment.'

My time fishing with Hilding come to an end mainly because of greedy shop owners. We'd deliver the fish to the Casuarina Shopping Centre on ice, ready to sell, getting about $3.00 to $4.00 per kilogram. The same fish was quite often sold for five times that money, and one day we told them to go and catch their own bloody fish. The same situation remains today: the primary producer, whether on land or at sea, is exploited terribly, and most of the population is convinced the supermarkets produce all their food. There was also a problem with illegal fishermen. When caught in Australian waters, their boats were confiscated and burnt, and their catches sold on the local market for a reduced price. When this happened, we got next to nothing.

CHAPTER 13

# Back to the Homeland

It was time for something different. I decided to take my whole family to Sweden in 1992. My Dad was not in the best of health, and I wanted him to see my son, Richard, who was his only grandson bearing the Peterson name. I'm glad I did, because I was able to see the amazed faces of my children as they were sitting at the kitchen window watching all the different animals, none of which they had seen in real life before. There were deer and hare, and badgers fed under the same cherry trees they'd been climbing earlier in the day, stuffing themselves full of juicy berries. We went across the lake and looked at some old Viking ruins. These fortifications had been built to keep enemies out, and at some time, would have been high enough to give protection. Now, a thousand years or so later, the highest points stood at only a couple of feet. Interestingly, when this fortress was built, there had been a lot of edible berries and nuts planted, no doubt for food when the fortress was under siege. The different berries and fruit would have been welcome, and there were a lot of hazelnuts growing there very densely. Because of this, no other species had been able to take root. Inside the wall, it was all hazelnuts, while outside, there was pine, fir, birch, alder, aspen, and several other species.

When I started school, we went on an excursion there and were shown the rusty blob that had once been the iron loops the Viking ships used to tie up to. It was several metres above the current lake level and proves just how much the lake has receded. This lowering of the water level in the lakes has caused the extinction of freshwater eels. They need access to the Sargasso Sea to breed. The level of the sea is now higher than the lakes, so that connection is now broken.

During the time of the Vikings, there were pits dug to catch wild animals like bears and wolves. Some of those pits were close to my primary school. They would be dug at the end of a very narrow strip of land surrounded by water. The locals would arm themselves with hay forks and clubs, forming a line across this strip of land, and any animals standing between them and the pit would be driven into it. Men in boats easily killed any that tried to escape by taking to the lake.

The district we lived in used to have a lot of eels in the lakes when I was a kid, but today, there are none. Because of the low water level, the waterways that once connected the lake to the sea are silted up, and since the eels need access to the Sargasso Sea to spawn, they have all died out. This whole district used to be underwater, and there are many remnants from the Vikings. In one paddock belonging to our neighbour, there are a great number of Viking graves. They used to bury their more important people in their ships and outline the shape of the ships with stones. Many of the graves are no longer visible; the stones marking the graves were the right size for laying the foundation of many of the local houses and sheds and were used for that purpose. One bridge has a large runestone in its foundation.

## Chapter 13: Back to the Homeland

The Vikings from the area where I grew up went mainly east on their raids. There are many books written of their exploits, which I read as a young boy, and one tells of the search by a young Viking for his elder brother. When a first son was born, the father went out into the forest and picked out enough trees to build a house, mainly pine and spruce. He would belt those trees with a big mallet to severely bruise them. This would increase the flow of the resin as the trees were trying to heal themselves. The trees would die over a long period as the resin would act as a preserver, protecting the wood, which would have been more or less dry by the time the son came of age and wanted to build his own home. Some of the buildings that were treated that way are still standing, several hundred years later, without any insect damage. There is one place in Russia where a comet came down hundreds of years ago in a pine forest, the enormous pressure caused when it hit the ground had the same effect as the mallet. The trees died over a long period, and yet the forest is still standing, preserved by the resin.

Once the firstborn son turned twenty and had built his own home, he had to prove himself by staging a raid on a foreign country, using his own ship and crew. This story is about one raid to the east, through Russia and following the rivers south to Turkey. The Vikings had a big base in Istanbul, one of which had successfully raided some wealthy establishments but failed to return. When his younger brother came of age, he decided to go looking for him. On the way, he met a merchant ship in the Baltic Sea, near an island by the name of Gotland. It was a big trading centre in those days. The people on the other ship signalled to them to pull alongside. 'We got a man onboard,' they said, 'that may belong to your part of the world; he is blind and has no tongue. He must have escaped capture after being severely tortured, but since he can't tell us anything, we stopped you in case you recognized him.'

The young Viking asked the man a lot of questions: 'If your answer is yes, nod your head. If no, shake it.'

The blind man became more and more frustrated until the young Viking asked him, 'Are you my brother, who left all those years ago from our village?'

The man nodded his head and started to cry. His younger brother returned to his village, and once at home tried to put together a picture of what had happened. He spent ages trying to formulate questions that could be answered by a nod or a headshake but to no avail.

The village carpenter came up with a brilliant idea: 'If I carve the runes in wood, he will be able to feel the shapes and tell his story that way.'

It worked. I consider this to be one of the first rudimentary forms of braille. The blind man told his younger brother that he was captured on his way home after a very successful raid but managed to hide his loot under some tree roots alongside one of the rivers. Once captured, he had his eyes burnt out and tongue cut off to stop him from escaping, and he was kept as a slave. The younger brother decided he would go back to see if he could find the treasure. He did, and it was still in top condition, and most of it would have been gold and silver. The Vikings were great admirers of jewellery and very skilful in making it.

I became involved in translating a book once, written in old Norse, describing how to make gold and silver jewellery. I had a friend who belonged to a lapidary club and had come across this old handbook. It was a surprise to find that a lot of words my Dad used were, in fact, old Norse, which helped me to translate quite a portion. I also discovered that the Vikings were very

## Chapter 13: Back to the Homeland

skilled artisans, and there were a lot of illustrations showing how they were making flexible gold chains, for instance

When reflecting with my family about Mum's childhood, a common theme was that the size of your bank account always decided justice in those days. I can remember the story of my grandfather on Mum's side. He was a constable in the local police force and among his many different duties was fine collection. One day when he got back to the police station with the day's collection, he was told by the sergeant in charge that he would have to wait to next week to get a receipt for the money he'd collected since the receipt book was empty. When he reminded the sergeant the following week, he told my grandfather he couldn't remember ever receiving any money from him. Having been the victim myself of corrupt legal procedures, I totally believe my mother's recollection

Grandfather was accused of stealing the money and sacked from the police force. He had a big family to feed, no other skills, and nobody would employ a thief anyway. It was now a matter of survival. The family had a pet dog, the only thing that could be called a luxury and whom all the kids loved. The fact was that even the scraps that had been fed to the dog were now needed to keep the family alive, and Axel, my grandfather, had no choice but to take it down into the bush and kill it. He was a truly lovely man who used to spend a lot of time at our farm. I suspect one strong reason for this was his keenness for fishing, and he spent a lot of time on the lake largely to get away from my grandmother, Elin, who was the complete opposite of him. Axel was a giant of a man, and law enforcers were picked on size and power in those days, whereas my grandmother was a very small woman. The difference in size between the two of them was often the subject of ridicule. One day at the local store, one of the customers asked, 'Axel, how come you don't kill that little woman of yours in bed?'

My grandfather was a very witty man. He turned to the man asking the question and replied, 'Have you ever heard of an elephant killing a flea by laying on it?'

When he was kicked out of the police force and was finding it very hard to find a job, he started repairing shoes in a little shed not much bigger than a pantry. He also kept bees and collected a fair bit of honey. I took my family to see the little hut; it was still there in 1992. He was such a happily-natured man and could be heard singing at the top of his voice while working. He used to put together some amazing ballads about the hobnobs in society, like the bastard sergeant who had been the cause of his sacking. I know that my oldest brother had some of his ballads taped. He played them to me many years ago.

My mother's family was big, with four boys and four girls. The boys would spend some very cold evenings in the woodshed where they had a wood lathe set up. It was hand-operated, so one person would turn a crank handle while another one would use the lathe. They were all very artistic and were well-known violin and boat builders. Yngve, the oldest one, was employed at a boat-building yard where he became a designer and builder of luxury yachts, all without any proper training or education. There was a lot of artistic ability on Mum's side.

Art in those days was viewed with suspicion, but my uncles were able to combine their gift with practicality. I share the stories of my grandfather and his family to show the reality of life in those days and is only a small sample of the treatment of the poor. This was still very obvious when I left Sweden, with the wealthy and well-bred people having their own benches in church next to the altar - closer to God? Some of them were the

## Chapter 13: Back to the Homeland

biggest sinners around! I've always been very much against this segregation.

One of the toughest parts of this trip home was seeing Dad so frail. In my youth, every day Dad was working close to home in the timber, I'd be there helping him after school. We worked a lot together in the forest and were pretty well matched, physically. To see him living in an institution for old and dependent people was very difficult. He'd been too hard for Mum to care for at home, and she was not in the best health herself at the time. He also had dementia. I remembered sitting at the kitchen table. He looked at my son intently and said to my brother, Olle, 'That is a fine boy you have got there.'

My brother said, 'You got it all wrong, Dad, he's not mine, he is Bill's.'

Dad snapped back to reality for a brief second, 'That is typical of you, you have always blamed your brother for everything,' he roared, and then he was gone.

Dad was being fed food that had no taste, with salt and sugar missing from most of it, the excuse given that it wasn't good for his health. The fact Dad was dying didn't matter to the people who were caring for him. The madness of this health regime was brought home to me by my sister Clearry, who had brought some fresh strawberries from our farm and given Dad a plateful with fresh cream. She was told the cream was no good for Dad; it contained too much fat. She told them to mind their own business. I'd like to point out that this was not an isolated incident. It has been revealed that here in Australia, people that have been depending on institutions to care for them in their old age have been terribly neglected, and it was coming to the fore in 2020.

Sometimes I'd pick him up from the old peoples home and bring him to his real home, our family farm. It was pretty hard going as he had dementia, and on one occasion, when I dropped him back to the aged care facility he was living at, he got stuck into me. 'You came here to take me home for the day, but before we got anywhere, you're putting me back in my room again. Make up your bloody mind!'

He was very upset. It was the last time I saw him and the first time he received a hug from me out of compassion. I hope he felt it, but I felt a great sadness, all those years without any close contact.

When he was home on the farm, he would eat as if he'd never seen food before, while at the institution, he hardly touched it. This is, I believe, standard practice at institutions worldwide: if you give the older people tasteless food, they don't eat. They become weak, listless, and stay in bed most of the time, making them easy to check on and the institutions cheap to run. There was one instance where Dad got up during the night to go to the loo: he couldn't get out of bed. The nursing staff had put a wooden frame around it, the purpose being to stop Dad from walking just in case he fell. No one told Dad. Waking up and finding a fence around your bed would be quite alarming for anybody. Dad panicked and hurt himself. After another similar incident, he hurt himself badly and was taken to hospital in an ambulance. I believe he died shortly after.

It's terrible to see a man you once raced to keep up with reduced to a commodity.

CHAPTER 14

# Paving a New Path

On our return from Sweden, we decided to move to Gin Gin, Queensland, where I had bought a block of land with some of the money the insurance had paid after my accident. I intended to start a blasting service for the locals while building on the land I had bought. Things didn't work out, however, and after a couple of months of unemployment, I took a job cutting timber for a company at Beerburrum, about fifty kilometres north of Brisbane. This was something I was familiar with, and if you were prepared to work hard, you made fabulous money.

I was cutting timber on contract, and my son Richard came over and gave me a hand after he finished school. He stayed a few months, just long enough to save up money for a car and long enough for the girls in WA to miss him. It was really good to have him working with me, he was a very hard worker, and it was the longest time we'd ever had together. We grew quite close. The mill we supplied changed hands, and the new owners cut our earnings dramatically. We still had a year or more left of our contract but were told that we'd have to take them to court if we wanted that sort of money—this from one of the world's biggest timber companies, who were basically untouchable.

I leased a little portable mill and started doing a lot of salvage work. I quickly found out this country wastes more than half of the forest harvesting, and I started a timber salvage operation, first in WA and later in Queensland. I was flat out salvaging logs that would have otherwise been chipped or burnt. A lot of the timber salvaged were pine trees, and I'd get the timber treated against termites and rot and sell it as garden sleepers, fencing or building material.

During this period, I met a woman who had a water pump for sale and owned a farm some distance away. Upon hearing that the lease on the farm I was living on was running out, she asked me if I would be interested in leasing her farm. It had been lying idle for about ten years, having being used for pineapple growing. The property had a large creek running through it and an unlimited irrigation permit. This seemed an opportunity too good to miss.

There was a lot of cleaning up to be done, with some of the land having pine trees growing on it which had self-seeded from an adjoining stand of pines. There were big ridges of dirt, topsoil which had been pushed up to get at the deep layers of sand underneath: some sand mining had taken place in the past. It was also overgrown with weeds, of which some varieties were very hard to get rid of. There had been some fires burning deep holes in the peat which was present in places, holes too deep for an ordinary wheel tractor to drive over. Finally, after a lot of heavy machinery had been over the area I was going to lease, I could get over it with a wheeled tractor and put some crops in.

The locals had told me that nothing would grow after pineapples had been grown, because a certain poison that was

## Chapter 14: Paving a New Path

used to keep weeds under control would kill everything except pineapples. However, the owner assured me no poison had been used on her farm, which was good enough for me. The first crop of tomatoes was the highest yielding crop I'd ever grown. This, despite the landowner telling me that the ground was useless. 'We didn't even grow pineapples on it!' she said. 'The best ground is next to Lagoon Creek, and I would advise you to move the irrigation pipes over there. It made sense since that would mean a shorter distance to pump the water.'

This, however, was a big mistake. Everything I planted died. I'd been growing potatoes in WA for years, yet they took ages to emerge when I planted them here. When I finally put a fork into the ground to find out why, I got a shock; instead of growing up to the surface, the potatoes had grown the stems underneath. They looked like spaghetti. It was evident to me that something was very wrong with the soil, so I took some samples for analysis. It was a costly business, and I was putting a lot of money into this farm with very little or no return.

The results were staggering. The samples had been tested for a lot of different poisons. The reportable level, where the amount is considered toxic to the plant, is 0.5. All but the poison used for weed control in the pineapples came back with a reading below that number. The poison used in the pineapples, Diuron, came back with a reading of 4.9 or ten times the legally acceptable level. This poison was banned in Sweden in 1993 since it was thought to cause cancer. It was never allowed to be used in agriculture, only to sterilize the ground under power lines and along railway lines. It is, in fact, a soil sterilant, pineapples and sugarcane being just about the only plant tolerant to it. In areas with a lot of runoff from the pineapple farms, big gum trees and mangroves are dying from this poison. There is also anecdotal evidence of people having built on land previously used for pineapple growing and losing the fruit trees they'd planted once they reached a certain size because the roots had grown down to the groundwater. While it was banned in Australia in 2011, the ban was rescinded by APVMA in 2012.

The reaction of the authorities supposedly responsible for the use of dangerous chemicals when I contacted them was an impressive display of passing the buck. It took a long time to find out how this poison worked and its lifespan. A lecturer at a university in Townsville told me that traces of it had been found around the Great Barrier Reef, some fifty kilometres out to sea, and even small amounts had even been found in rainwater tanks. There was the answer to something that had puzzled me. Every time I irrigated the crops or after a heavy rain, the crop would die or look like they were suffering. Once in the groundwater, it could be there for life. Despite the serious implications, my experience indicated that nobody in authority cares. What if generations down the track find out that this is affecting people's health, like Agent Orange? Today, many people like to be self-sufficient, growing their own vegetable and pumping water from wells. It is a scary thought, knowing that the water may be polluted. Some of the housing estates north of Brisbane have been built on old pineapple farms, with the homeowners having trees dying once they get their roots into a certain depth. This was the reason, of course, why my first crop of tomatoes was such a success: in the owner's own words, there had never been any pineapples grown on that particular piece of ground, and consequently, no poison had been used.

While I was trying to get some crops established on the land I was leasing, I had a machine built that I'd invented. The idea for this machine had been in my head since the age of seventeen.

## Chapter 14: Paving a New Path

I was digging a drain, my first job since leaving home, through a peat swamp. Once the peat had dried, we tried to spread it on the paddock so that we could put a crop in, but it proved impossible. Peat becomes very fluffy and light once it's dry, and the implements available at the time would not touch it. Rotary hoes were not invented then. I spotted an old bit of wooden construction on the side of the paddock. It was a wood frame with a couple of rollers mounted inside. The rollers had rows of metal spikes sticking out of them. This got my imagination going. This was the first such implement that I had seen. *Could I use it for breaking the dry peat by rolling this machine over it?* We repaired it and drove it back and forth a few times. The spikes broke the peat down well enough for us to spread it.

Sweden has been farmed for over 3,000 years, and I'm convinced this type of implement had been used by the Vikings. The machine I designed, which I've named the Wiking Rollavator, is a great improvement on the one that I had used as a seventeen-year-old. It has three rollers inside a frame, each one with eight rows of triangle-shaped blades. Those blades intersect at ground level, which means when the blades from the first roller are coming out of the ground, they come into contact with the blades on the following roller going down. This happens horizontally at the surface. The result is the topsoil, where all the microbic and humus forming activity takes place, stays on the top, providing the shallow feeding roots of the plants with nourishment. This is in stark contrast with the rotary hoe, for instance, which mixes all the soil to whatever depth it is working. One pass with a rotary hoe dilutes the topsoil that has taken generations of farmers to create.

There is no other machine like the Wiking Rollavator that can do the same job for the same cost. The first prototype I made cost about $2000 in materials and was all homemade from scrap metal. I had to make it to prove the concept would work. I designed the machine, and a good friend of mine, Mick Smith, took on the job of constructing the prototype at his engineering works in Caboolture. We found the wear and tear are minimal as the working parts utilise slow-motion, and the speed that it can be operated at is amazing.

Given the worldwide concern about air pollution, a lot of it from fuel consumption, any reduction in hours used to cultivate a paddock must be welcome. There is no noise and very little dust, which is another serious factor in operating a lot of machinery. In Australia, cities like Melbourne are choked with dust storms every year. A lot of that dust is topsoil, caused by the lack of fibre matter in the surface. We had one of those severe storms on my farm one year in Western Australia that blew the soil off the potato crop. On the windy side, the potatoes laid bare and went green, becoming unsuitable for anything. This sort of weather was never heard of when I first came to Australia.

My dad once told me about a next-door neighbour in Sweden, an animal lover that the locals used to poke fun at. There was a saying that when 'Kalle i Mantorp' ploughed with the horses, the sun shone through the tilth. I asked what his crops looked like. 'No different to the rest of us,' Dad said. I thought about this quite a bit. Why flog the hell out of your horses if the crop did not improve?

Every time a paddock is ploughed, there is soil brought to the surface that is of little use to most plants, diluting the rich top layer of soil where the humus and microorganisms are located and where the feeding roots are getting all the nutrients. It is therefore very important to keep the topsoil at the top and keep building on to it to give the plants the best growing conditions.

## Chapter 14: Paving a New Path

The Rollavator can also be used for cultivating the paddocks before the winter. In the northern hemisphere, opening up the soil deep down and mixing all straw materials at the surface means the early spring sun will start off the bacteria and microorganism activity a lot earlier than in the straw that been ploughed in deep. Deep ripping of the soil also has the benefit of collecting water from the melting snow and ice.

We have had this cultivator at work with the strawberry growers here in Queensland. One six-acre patch that used to take the grower six hours to cultivate with a rotor hoe was done in just over an hour with the Rollavator. That is 80% less time in the paddock, 80% less fuel consumption and consequently the same reduction in air pollution. It is virtually dust-free when operating this implement; the lack of dust in the air was quite obvious. Since we've had two very dry years in a row in this part of Queensland, it brings home the benefits of any rain being soaked up by the ripped ground rather than running off the surface, creating flooding. Another expensive result of the water running off is the loss of topsoil and the nutrients there in the high country lacking in moisture and fertility, the low country getting too much.

The benefit of this machine leaving so much mulch on the top cannot be overestimated. It helps absorb rain and retain moisture. It also encourages worm activity, which is of enormous benefit to the plants. This machine can also be fitted with a seedbox and planting tubes for seedlings, so cultivation and planting can be done in one operation. Where I farmed in Queensland, the forestry department ran a trial on fertilisers to understand which one best suited young trees. Worm casting out-performed all the rest.

I planted pumpkins in 2019, and after spraying the weeds, I seeded the paddock with oats at a very high rate. I irrigated for a week and the oats came up very thick, stopping any weeds from germinating. Once the oats got to about 20mm high, I sprayed a small patch every couple of meters with Fusilade, which only kills grass, and planted the pumpkin seed. While the pumpkin seeds were coming up, the sprayed patches of oats were dying off. When the whole oat crop was 500mm high, I sprayed the whole paddock with Fusilade, within a month all the oats were dead. I now had a thick layer of mulch covering the pumpkin crop and no weeds. Because of this mulch, despite the driest season for many years, the crop was about double that of the previous year and the worms are back.

Landline made the video of my machine March 2020. This machine proved it would be possible to eradicate weeds without killing half the world's population with all the toxic substances now used in weed control. It also proved to be incredibly efficient, cultivating the same area that was before done with a rotary hoe in less than a quarter of the time.

We have made some machines and sold a few, with a lot of interest shown by modern farmers who were using machinery like rotary hoes to smash any dirt into a texture fine enough to plant in. Farming practices of late enable the modern farmer the luxury of planting crops whenever his social calendar shows he has the time. This, however, is not the best way of managing the land.

As a boy, my brother and I would walk behind Dad when he was ploughing with the horses, and in a few metres, pick up enough worms to go fishing for a day. On my last visit to Sweden some years ago, I could not find a single worm. Because of modern farming, with no animals and thus no stable manure, the topsoil had deteriorated due mainly to a lack of organic matter. This has seen a proliferation of surface cracks and lots of weed. It

## Chapter 14: Paving a New Path

is hard to understand why the home gardener, who has realised the importance of the organic matter and are using mulch in ever-increasing quantity to improve the health of the soil, grasps this point, while it seems to have been missed by the people that are professionally relying on healthy soil for a living.

There were huge costs incurred while farming the land I had leased with all the deadly herbicide in the ground. For the last couple of crops I put in, I was paying by credit card since it was impossible to grow enough crops just to cover costs. As I was planning on commercialising my invention, I needed a clean record, and there was no other way out except coming to an agreement with my creditors and paying part of my debts. This meant I had to scrape together every dollar available, leaving no money to spare for personal use. I ended up living in a corrugated iron shed—the very type of accommodation I'd had when first starting out in Australia, more than fifty years before.

Finding myself in these circumstances, completely without financial means, is pretty hard to take. Being duped by a fellow farmer and a charming woman to boot is also pretty hard to take. The property that I leased with all that poison in the ground is still lying idle. No one knows how long it will take to rid the soil of all the toxic substances that have been applied.

After I had the soil samples analysed, I started legal proceedings for compensation. This was a shocking experience for me. The authorities that are responsible for this terrible poison informed my lawyer that if their name appeared in court, they could more or less guarantee that I would get no compensation. The alternative was to settle outside court. I ended up with a pitiful amount. The small-time criminals are exposed in court. The big ones escape because of out-of-court settlements.

I have now reached a time in my life when the mental capacity, as feeble as it is, can be too much for the rest of the body. One step I have taken towards a more stress-free life is to move to South Australia to be with my daughter, Anne-Britt and my son-in-law, Neil. At the time of writing this book, I am in a holding pattern thanks to COVID-19, with the coronavirus disrupting so many lives and, of course, taking many.

CHAPTER 15

# A Change of Pace

When you get to my age of almost seventy-six, the circle of friends and family becomes smaller and smaller, which is quite depressing. Life, however, goes on unfortunately at an ever-increasing speed, or so it seems.

My last visit to Sweden in 2013 was very busy. I stayed with an old friend of mine, Thorgny and his partner Leni for a couple of days. He is a retired draftsman and offered to help with some drawings for parts to be added to my invention. It was a very enjoyable stay. I met up with the guy I worked for when I left Sweden, Yngve Pettersson, and had dinner there. It was quite sad; he's not in good health, having suffered from Parkinson's disease for many years. However, it was nice to see him and his lovely wife, Ingegerd. I stayed with my elder brother, whom I've told of earlier, and with my sister Clearry and her husband, Wello. There was also time for a visit to my old Agriculture College to talk about the Wiking Rollavator and a reunion with a fellow student from my time there, Sirja, and her husband, Janne Lillmasen. My cousin, Lasse Johansson, picked me up from the train station and delivered me back to my sister's place after an amazing dinner at his home. It was very enjoyable since I hadn't had the opportunity to speak to his lovely wife, Eva, before. I've also met with four of my nieces: Kitty, Zenitha, Maria, Malin, and their kids. It's been too many years and such happy meetings.

There was also time to meet with Ann-Britt, my brother's first wife (my daughter is named after her), who was a perfect hostess while I was visiting Sweden in 1973. I was the waste bin: any leftovers after meals were my job to finish off. She served a delicious dinner, and I had a nice afternoon with her and her daughters. Malin has been visiting Australia twice in the last few years, the others I haven't seen since 1997.

One visit that I will treasure for the rest of my life is the time I spent with Eva. She is the most beautiful girl I have ever seen, and I spoke about her at the beginning of the book. She was just as I had imagined her, the little bit extra that has remained with me all my life. Maybe it is the same for everyone, that first love, but I like to think mine was special. If everything turns out as planned for a change, maybe I will see her again sooner than I think.

The stay with Olle and Anita was amazing. At our age, it's been so much safer to be together, no worries of being pushed into deep water when you can't swim or using my name in vain when in trouble with girls. Anita's children are just fantastic and are all very happy and easy to get on with. I enjoyed my trip with Nicke and also her sister Maggan, and my favourite, her mother, Maj. Staying in such harmonious surrounding, I couldn't help but compare it to my own two marriages and realised it takes two to tango.

I would like to add something about my marriages here: I don't think I was cut out to be married. My first marriage to Barbara Martin was one of convenience, more on my part than

## Chapter 15: A Change of Pace

that of my wife, maybe. It was a marriage of hormones as much as anything. Looking back, she was much too young and never really had a normal adolescence. She was a very capable young lady who deserved better. But such is life; it would be so easy to make things perfect with hindsight. Without the help of her family, however, life for me would have been so much harder. There is one thing that I always will be grateful for: the two beautiful, loving children she gave me. I hope her old age will be as rewarding as mine.

My second marriage to Andy was completely different, with both parties of mature age and no children from our marriage. Mind you, mixing children from previous marriages takes formidable strength and effort. Regardless of age, thinking that things would be easier because of our previous experiences turned out to be somewhat off target. However, my second wife, a well-educated, intelligent woman with the sort of humour only the English have, was responsible for our marriage lasting as long as it did. She was of great support to me during many hard years, and remarkably, we've remained very good friends long after we divorced. This relationship means a lot to me, as does the rekindled contact with her youngest daughter, Claire, after a twenty-five-year hiatus.

This seems a very short description of my time as a married man, or should I say part-time as a married man, but I'm no good at embroidery, so I will leave it at that except to state that a woman's role in everyday life is grossly underrated.

My last visit to Sweden was a whirlwind, meeting a lot of relations and friends from the air force and agriculture college. It was all possible through the effort of my sister Clearry and my brother Olle. The latter drove me everywhere. It was a very emotional trip to my country of birth, with the number of people known to me dwindling at an alarming rate and mainly due to the year they were made.

Some highlights were meeting my nieces and their wonderful kids, some for the first time. I also had the opportunity to show a video of my Wiking Rollavator to a large crowd of interested people. If things go well, I could be back in this beautiful green country pretty soon. There has been some extreme weather in Sweden over the summers. A lot of the country is dry. Many very light crops are already harvested; a lot of forests burned and dying, and up north, enormous areas have been burned out. This area right across the west to Norway has pine forests, making the people who manage the pine forests in Australia cry with envy: so many tall, limb-free trees.

During the last ten to fifteen years, I've been busy growing vegetables and making rustic timber furniture for the local market on the Sunshine Coast. During the delivery of a giant Camphor Laurel slab to a Kiwi lady, Judi, I met every man's dream woman. Judi went on to become my closest friend. 2020 was a terrible year, with COVID-19 putting a dampener on everybody's life, but out of nowhere came this bundle of energy into my life, and it has not been the same since. Judi has been pushing me to reunite with my daughter in South Australia, something I had been dreaming about for several years. The visits have been few since her wedding to Neil, but I'm here now, in a charming little country town by the name of Strathalbyn.

My daughter Anne-Britt was born in 1971, she was a very quiet baby, but we found out some weeks later that she had heart problems. One heart valve was faulty, which made the healthy one work too hard, causing cramps. She has had several heart operations but is celebrating her 50th birthday in 2021. Her future health prognosis is promising, and we both have a lot

## Chapter 15: A Change of Pace

of family life to catch up on. I will be working on getting my invention marketed while staying with this loving couple. My daughter has designed my website, wikingrollavator.com, which showcases my machine. Many grape growers in South Australia think my machine is the answer to their prayers. Ann-Britt has a well-established copywriting business and is the prime motor when it comes to the business end.

I am looking forward to an exciting old age developing this machine and getting onto farms to transform the way modern farmers utilise their land and bring methods back to chemical-free solutions.

Despite all the downfalls in the structure of society since I first arrived in this country, it's hard to find anywhere else that I would rather be. I'm looking forward to spending the years I have got left with close family, a luxury not enjoyed for a very long time. I also hope that there will be some readers that can benefit from my story.

I'd like to finish with a poem that reflects my thoughts about my life:

I realise now that all along,
I made decisions that were wrong.
I sailed away across the sea,
And left the girl that meant so much to me.
But I was young and free, I had no cares back then,
So many girls were mine, but still a lonely man.
I used to think I was the one who mattered most,
But I was wrong.
The people that I didn't see,
They were the ones who mattered most to me.
The worst day, as I recall,

I came home late, where are they all?
There are no kids, nor there a wife,
I am alone, so cruel is life.
But in the lonely night, when in my bed I turn,
It becomes clear to me, I am of small concern.
But better not to rue my fate,
Or dream of things that could have been … too late.

www.ingramcontent.com/pod-product-compliance
Lightning Source LLC
Chambersburg PA
CBHW071619080526
44588CB00010B/1188